WHERE DOES IT HURT?

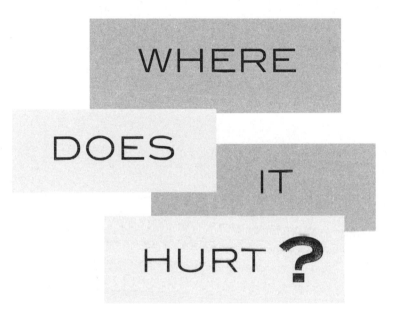

WHERE DOES IT HURT?

AN ENTREPRENEUR'S GUIDE TO FIXING HEALTH CARE

JONATHAN BUSH

WITH STEPHEN BAKER

PORTFOLIO / PENGUIN

PORTFOLIO / PENGUIN

Published by the Penguin Group
Penguin Group (USA) LLC
375 Hudson Street
New York, New York 10014

USA | Canada | UK | Ireland | Australia | New Zealand | India | South Africa | China
penguin.com
A Penguin Random House Company

First published by Portfolio / Penguin, a member of Penguin Group (USA) LLC, 2014

LIBRARY OF CONGRESS CATALOGING-IN-PUBLICATION DATA
Bush, Jonathan, 1969– author.
Where does it hurt? : an entrepreneur's guide to fixing health care / Jonathan Bush ; with Stephen Baker.
p. ; cm.
Includes index.
ISBN 978-1-59184-677-2
I. Baker, Stephen, 1955 November 15– author.   II. Title.
[DNLM: 1. Delivery of Health Care—United States—Personal Narratives.   2. Health Care
Reform—United States—Personal Narratives.   W 84 AA1]
RA413.5.U5
362.1'0425—dc23   2014004253

Printed in the United States of America
1   3   5   7   9   10   8   6   4   2

Set in ITC Baskerville MT Std
Designed by Alissa Rose Theodor

For Mandi,
who knows better than most the pain of change
and the beauty of surviving it

CONTENTS

CONTENTS

FOREWORD

This is one of the most important and engaging books about health care I have ever read. I love Jonathan's ideas, of course, but it is his perspective that is so unique. My books examine problems from a rarefied, conceptual, top-down perspective. Jonathan's perspective on heath care occurs from the bottom up. It is refreshing. Over the years, he has been an ambulance driver, an army medic, and a consultant. He has seen firsthand the local and national politics of health care. He was initially a failed entrepreneur with a great idea, covered with scabs and wounds from wringing out reimbursements from insurance companies and wrestling with the status quo. Now Jonathan is the successful CEO of a marvelous and important health care IT company.

Let me offer an analogy for what Jonathan brings to the discussions about curing our health care system. For much of the 1800s in America where there ostensibly was freedom of religion, tens of thousands of members of the Mormon Church were persecuted: hunted, killed, and driven from their farms and homes. To escape this persecution their leaders led them to the uninhabited desert in the West, where they hoped they could worship as they chose. The exodus of these good people—penniless because they had been stripped of their possessions by their persecutors—is one of the most gripping episodes in the history of America. They organized themselves into "companies" of hundreds, so they could protect and help each other deal with the never-ending dangers they faced on the trail. Four of my great-grandparents made this trek, walking across the plains with their food and possessions in a covered wagon or a two-wheeled handcart.

In 1947, to commemorate the hundredth anniversary of the first company of pioneers entering into the Salt Lake Valley, a leader of our church, J. Reuben Clark, gave a powerful talk entitled "To Them of the Last Wagon." He observed that almost all of the historical accounts of the exodus took the perspective of the leaders who were at the front of the long trains of wagons. To them, the air was clear and the wind from the western plains cooled their sweaty brows on sultry July afternoons. When they came across a knoll they could stop the company so that the leaders could survey what lay ahead. To those of the last wagon, however, the journey was decidedly different. Every day consisted of breathing the dust raised by scores of wagons in front of them. They walked twenty miles daily through the manure deposited by hundreds of oxen that were pulling the wagons ahead of them. They were last because the ox team that pulled their wagon was the smallest and leanest and weakest. But when those in the last wagon saw a broken wagon ahead on the trail, they instinctively offered their help. When the last wagon broke, or they were sick, or an ox went lame, however, most of the rest of the company didn't notice because they were looking at their own problems ahead. The heartache, determination, courage, and perspective of those in the last wagon were very different from the experience of the leaders at the front.

In *Where Does It Hurt?* Jonathan chronicles the people who occupy the last wagon in health care. These are the patients who don't have access to the best care. They are caregivers and entrepreneurs who could give so much more and better care than they are allowed if they weren't chained to a broken system. Those in the first wagon write the legislation and regulation. They debate health care in courts and legislatures. Many of their compromises and side deals fill the air with self-centeredness, complexity, ambiguity, overhead costs, and contested, delayed, and partial reimbursement. The lives of those in the last wagon are very different from the "visionaries" in the front.

Thankfully, Jonathan has experience driving wagons in both the back and the front. He has a wonderful perspective of the entire wagon train. Jonathan has dedicated his life and his company to helping those of the last wagon in health care do their jobs in the best way possible and creating new opportunities for those entrepreneurs who are willing to take risks.

I love to listen to Jonathan talk: His narratives come a mile per minute. His illustrations and metaphors help me envision the problems and their solutions clearly. And he is very, very funny. You will be able to hear Jonathan's voice as you read this book. It is an easy, insightful, and entertaining read.

Jonathan, thank you for writing this book—for what it says and how you say it.

Clayton Christensen, Harvard Business School

JANUARY 2014

WHERE DOES IT HURT?

INTRODUCTION

It's a steamy summer night in New Orleans in 1990. I'm twenty-one years old and gunning an ambulance down Bienville Avenue, toward Charity Hospital. My uncle is president of the United States and my cousin will take over the same job in a decade. Big things are expected of me. But I've always had trouble succeeding along traditional Bush family lines. Surrounded by a brother and cousins who are outstanding athletes, I have trouble throwing and catching. I'm also dyslexic and struggle at school. I fidget in classrooms, and my mind wanders. So now, between my sophomore and junior years of college, I'm exploring a new path. It involves doing good by running red lights and crashing through windshields to rescue people. I love it.

Charity Hospital has what is widely considered a crack trauma unit, perhaps the best in the country. Located in the heart of America's murder capital, the New Orleans team gets loads of do-or-die practice. But the seventy-five-year-old man stretched out behind me right now isn't an emergency case. He just feels bad. I think he has high blood pressure. The shootings every night in his neighborhood can't help. So he called 911. He met us on his stoop, fully dressed and carrying an overnight bag. He is taking what amounts to a $400 cab ride paid for by

Medicaid. (I joke that I'm driving a *cab-u-lance*.) When we get there, the triage nurses will point him toward the waiting room, where he'll probably sit for hours, while doctors rush to treat the stab and gunshot victims we haul in. Finally, when a doctor gets a couple of minutes between turns to see this old man, he'll give him a prescription and send him on his way. This visit costs the system hundreds, even thousands, of dollars. The patient clogs up the hospital and gets rotten service. And he'll be back in a week or two. After all, his condition is *chronic*.

Now imagine for a moment how dramatically this interaction with a patient would change if hospitals like Charity had to run like a normal business. The hospital (which, incidentally, was destroyed fifteen years later by Hurricane Katrina) would have to turn its business model upside down, because virtually no one could afford the bills. Even in this impoverished nook of America, rates run about the same as those at the Ritz or the Beverly Wilshire. It's thousands of dollars per day, plus charges for incidentals, from bandages to syringes. The sad truth is that in hospitals we pay for a Ritz experience, but the service we get is below the YMCA.

No, the business model of this hospital, and practically every one I've encountered since, is predicated on mysterious and outrageous charges that someone else, either an insurance company or the government, will eventually pay or haggle down. A competitive market is nowhere in sight. There is almost no consideration of the patient as a customer with choices, someone who could conceivably compare prices and service and value. In our convoluted health care system, the insurance company is the customer, and the patient—even a poor one like the guy who's getting ready to climb out of my ambulance—is a widget to be processed, administered, and billed for. From the system's perspective, he's a potential stream of revenue.

Now if this were a real business, like a pizzeria or a nail salon, the hospital would have to seriously rethink its pricing model. Instead of pegging its invoices to Medicare or Medicaid reimbursements, or whatever it can get from private insurers, it would instead have to focus on the gentleman in my backseat as a customer. The service he needs at this stage in his life is not emergency care, but maintenance. In a free market, maintenance comes out of the customer's pocket. Even in poor neighborhoods, drivers pay Jiffy Lube $39.95 for an oil change. Could an entrepreneur carve out a business by offering service at a similar price for hypertension or diabetes?

That's what I wonder as I patrol the steamy streets of New Orleans. I do the math. The hospital pays me $9 an hour (with no health insurance) to drive this ambulance. In a month or two, for a few thousand dollars, they could train me as a medic. Let's say they bump me up to $13, equip me with a van, and send me around to pay house calls on the chronically ill. These people would get better care. It would cost a fraction as much. It could be the seed of a business. But you can't expect hospitals and health plans to pursue such schemes. They're not traditional businesses, and they don't have to think like one. Many of their executives are faring just fine within the jury-rigged, price-fixed status quo. It's gushing dollars, with both buyers and sellers profiting from rising prices. Why change a thing?

Well, for lots of reasons. The status quo in health care is threatening to bankrupt our economy. It counts for nearly the entirety of our recent economic growth, if that's what you choose to call the mountain of health care IOUs we're writing. It's gobbling up money that otherwise would go into wage hikes and productive investments. We spend more than twice as much per capita for medical care as citizens of other rich countries, and we aren't any healthier. In fact, life expectancy for both men and women in the United States doesn't even crack the top twenty, worldwide. If the concept of customer satisfaction comes up in the industry, it's usually as a laugh line. If there were any choice, if people could shop for medical care, many would no doubt pick other options. But health care doesn't work like a normal industry, and it holds one trump card that grocery stores, coffee shops, and online retailers can't match: It can save our lives.

Yes, it's true. Doctors and nurses can and do save lives. So do the miracle drugs and space-age devices. Saving lives is what attracted me and millions of others to the industry. But that's no reason for an entire industry to get a pass on the market economy. In fact, it's by returning to a real marketplace that we can create the health industry we want, deserve, and can afford. And here the bad news actually has a silver lining. From an entrepreneur's point of view, there's something highly appealing, almost intoxicating, about waste and dysfunction in the industry. Think about it. If one fifth of the economy, about $2.7 trillion, gushes into a chaotic industry that is vital to our well-being and widely loathed, mightn't there be an opportunity for someone to offer great service, low prices, and convenience? In short, someone who runs health care like a business that appeals to customers? From a business point of view, health care is the new oil. Those who can dig down through the morass of rules, paperwork, and bureaucratic obstacles can find new markets. Gushers! They'll be the new wildcatters.

That's been my opinion and fervent hope for my entire adult life. I know it can happen. I've seen it, albeit on a small scale. And I fully believe that this market awakening represents the great hope for rescuing health care in America. It hinges on companies treating health care like a normal business and competing with each other. This process, strange as it might sound, involves market strategies and competitive pricing. Convenience and customer service will be a huge battleground, as will competition for statistically better results. The winners will innovate. They'll have no choice. And they'll be rewarded with heaping helpings of the fuel that drives markets: profits. This entrepreneurial trend in health care is already stirring.

I've been in the fray my whole career. A year after my return from New Orleans, Saddam Hussein's army invaded Kuwait. I plunged back into health care by enlisting in the U.S. Army to become a medic. It was my way of serving my country and my uncle George while also digging deeper into the industry (and avoiding a really big term paper at Wesleyan). After further education and a brief and unsuccessful tour as a consultant, I rejected wise counsel from sensible friends and committed the folly of launching a health care start-up. It was a set of birthing clinics in San Diego. I'm probably not giving away anything to tell you that it floundered, and then failed.

But something funny happened on the way down. To deal with the complexity of insurance reimbursements, we had created a software program for billing. We set it up on a digital network that was creating a sensation at the time. It was called the Internet. We soon saw that, while our birthing business was crashing, investors were all too happy to pour millions into our technology. So in 1998, we dropped birthing and became a back-office company, athenahealth. Since then, we have grown into a corporation worth more than $4 billion (Nasdaq: ATHN) I'm cofounder and CEO. Our cloud-based service handles much of the paperwork, billing, and electronic patient records for more than fifty thousand medical providers nationwide. Athenahealth thrives because we fulfill the mission we laid out at the very beginning: We handle the busywork that doctors absolutely hate—the stuff they suck at.

Through this on-the-job education, I have developed ideas about how to remake health care in America— or at least how to start. The Affordable Care Act—commonly known as Obamacare—is widely referred to as health care "reform." But it has focused the nation's attention largely on the demand side of the issue: providing health care for another 30 million or 40 million people. Most of the reforms, however, were watered down by lobbyists protecting the incumbents. So we're still left with fundamental questions around the supply side, namely how we can ensure affordable, quality care at something less than ruinous cost. If we plow ahead with the status quo, with health care costs rising higher than economic growth year after year, we'll soon confront choices that range from depressing to disastrous. Either we pay more for health care, even though we're doling out far more than other rich countries, or we consume less of it. It looks that simple. But it does not have to be.

I'm convinced that the true fix requires a revolution. It must stir market forces that have been virtually pulseless for the last half century. This process will make health care friendlier for consumers, giving them more choices, and also opening doors to entrepreneurs. That combination is the key for the innovation so desperately needed.

This change won't happen overnight. Nearly one fifth of the world's largest economy sustains legions of powerful stakeholders. They are already positioning themselves and lobbying to maintain the status quo, which sustains them. Standing center stage are hospitals. Their inpatient business alone gobbles up about as much money annually as the Department of Defense. I often get very angry about hospitals. They can be horribly inefficient and resistant to change. They overbill for routine procedures. And it irks me that so-called nonprofits make money hand over fist while enticing billionaires to donate marble and glass pavilions and sponsor research centers. I know one rich guy who—without even a trace of irony—left a chunk of his fortune for a hospital *waiting room*.

Still, the professionals in hospitals do wonderful and often inspiring work. If you face stage-three colon cancer or an exotic autoimmune disorder or, heaven forbid, find yourself attached Siamese-style to your twin, there's no better place to be than a name-brand American university research hospital. The feats surgeons pull off burnish their reputations as miracle workers and lifesavers. Many of them are brilliant virtuosos, even heroes, and I often can't help myself for loving and forgiving them their excesses. I certainly cannot blame them for defending their turf and their perks. How many people believe they should be paid less for what they do? What's more, the hospital-centric status quo, for all of its infuriating inefficiencies and excesses, is the only health care most of us know. So a lot of us cling to it as well. After all, it has kept all of us alive so far, and when it comes to survival, even a whiff of change is unwelcome.

So where will the disruptions start? They'll brew on the margins of the health care economy. They're already beginning in services that can be delivered by specialists that operate with the focus and efficiency of a factory. They aren't diagnosing exotic diseases or carrying out exploratory surgery. No, they're snapping X-rays and performing other routine procedures. Some of them are replacing knees and hips, and lasering eyes into focus. Others are bringing babies into the world. Their cost is lower and their service better. This trend will spread. And eventually it'll reach further into the operations and profit centers of hospitals. At the same time, health care businesses will continue to spread in areas associated with wellness, not disease. Think smart phone apps for diet and exercise, Weight Watchers classes, and the exercise studios for middle-aged women, Curves. These places hardly look revolutionary. But in the nonmarket of health care, they're committing revolutionary acts. They're focusing on services people need and, importantly, will pay for. This alone destabilizes and renovates niches of the health economy.

These revolutionaries, I should add, are out to make money. Profits. It's a dirty word among the corduroy-elbow crowd in the research hospitals and foundations. But just like every business, from Samsung to

Dogfish Head Brewery, this industry will grow and innovate by figuring out what we need and want, and selling it to us at prices we're able and willing to pay. Profit will drive this process if markets are allowed to emerge. It's the fuel for growth and innovation. The current health care economy, of course, has devised all kinds of subterfuge and roundabouts to drive revenue. Perhaps its greatest innovation is its nonbusiness model, which places a $2.7 trillion weight on our economy. We'd fare a lot better just by unshackling entrepreneurs and letting them shoot for profits in health care.

This sounds crass, I know, even heartless. But I would argue that the status quo is heartless. Doctors and nurses, many of them laboring for nonprofits, often might as well be chained to treadmills. To maximize revenue and service their patients, they must cram them into their schedules, dispatching them in ten or twelve minutes. And then, just to administer their highly regulated business, and to get paid, they turn to a nightmarish mountain of paperwork (much of it still real paper). So between the crowded waiting rooms and the paperwork, they fill their days, weeks, and years.

Sadly, they end up scrimping on the single most important interaction of their professional lives: the deep, one-on-one relationship between two people, the doctor and the patient. This is what is unique in health care. It is one person listening to another, and asking questions, and engaging the prodigious human mind, enriched and educated through college, grad school, residency, and years of valuable experience. During these encounters, the doctor focuses on one fellow human being with the goal of figuring out what ails this person and how to fix or alleviate it. It is this act of total presence—I would go so far as to call it a form of love—that should exist at the heart of health care. The promise of such connections led many doctors I know through ten years of medical-school hazing and marathon weekends in the libraries and labs. Beyond a comfortable lifestyle and steady work, they wanted careers offering meaning and service. But many doctors now find their time and efforts swallowed up by chores they hate. This deprives them and their patients of their deepest connections, and leads to discontent. A 2013 study by Jackson Healthcare shows that a stunning 59 percent of physicians would not recommend a medical career to young people. Atul Gawande, a surgeon and one of the most insightful writers about health care, says that primary care doctors across the country are suffering from burnout. "We've lost the joy in taking care of patients," he says.

How do we get it back, for them and for us? That's what this book is about. I've divided it into three parts. In the first section, I'm grappling with these challenges myself, from the ambulance in New Orleans and army boot camp to the birthing start-up in San Diego. Along this bumpy road, I come up with ideas for a renewed health care industry. The central one, of course, is to run it like a real business—with cost control, continuous improvement, smart use of technology, and fabulous customer service. Health care could learn a lot from Starbucks, Amazon, and Disney. The opening section closes a bit paradoxically: It follows my struggles, even as a nephew and cousin of presidents, to keep the government in Washington from inadvertently strangling our newborn data company.

In the second section, I map out the health care revolution, a Darwinian drama that's already under way. At the center of the turbulent ecosystem is the large research hospital. It's the jewel of American medicine, but fabulously expensive. Its business model is in trouble. Costs are through the roof. Inpatient stays are getting shorter. It tries to compensate by ushering in new streams of patients for overpriced tests and procedures. But as we'll see, there's new competition. Community hospitals are elbowing into their markets, and a new generation of start-ups is offering focused services at a fraction of the cost—and often

with better results. Even retailers, like Walgreens and Target, are jumping into the fray as they set up clinics in their stores.

I picture this ecosystem as rings of concentric circles. At each level,
competitors are targeting those on the inside, feasting on their inefficiencies and bloated prices. This spells trouble for research hospitals,
which occupy the center ring. But as I'll explain, there's also a pathway
to the future for them, even in a competitive marketplace. It won't be
easy, though, and some won't make it. The section closes with innovative medical practices, from Cambridge to the forests of the Adirondacks, that are remaking health care. They're doing it by doubling
down on primary care and expanding the notion of health care into
the rest of our lives, into diet, exercise, and mental health. This might
sound expensive, but they save money by keeping people out of the
hospital. This is great for business and, more important, far better for
their patients.

Data is the theme running through the third section. In the lumber-
ing health care industry that we have come to know in the last half
century, information is a scarce resource. Patients rarely have access to
their records. No one can hazard a guess as to what an operation, a
medicine, or even a Band-Aid might cost. Keeping this information
buttoned up benefits the incumbents, who thrive within what we might
call an ignorance economy. Some, as we'll see, are still attempting to
control their local markets by limiting access to data. Yet sooner or
later, data promises to turn this status quo on its head, ushering in a
slew of new digital start-ups and—most important—delivering vital
and timely information to the patients, or customers.

And what will they do with this information? It can be summed up
in a single word: *shopping*. This has to do with making choices. We
weigh countless options in the rest of our lives, but not nearly enough of
them in health care. Shopping, whether it's driven by an individual, a

retail buyer, or a wholesaler, creates the market, and the market responds with choices and innovation. What's more, in markets driven by shopping, losers figure out how and where to change their fortunes, or they disappear.

We need shopping, I believe, not only to fix health care, but also—and I know this may sound strange—to express our own humanity. Think about it. We shop for clothes to express our tastes and personality. We do the same for music and food. Some of us trick out our cars, put them on megawheels, or hang big, fuzzy dice from the mirror. We express who we are with these choices. And yet for the care of our bodies, for some of the most important decisions we make in life, we rely on a handful of menu options and lists drawn up by bureaucrats. What I want is for people to have a dizzying array of options in health care, so they can care for themselves and their loved ones in a way that suits them best, that makes them happy and proud. Some of the choices will be simple, of course, others delightfully convoluted. But in my vision, each of us will fashion the health care we want and deserve. We'll express ourselves.

As we proceed along our journey through life, each one of us has our encounters with the health care system. Some of them, no doubt, will be satisfying, but others far less so. The common tendency, I've found, is to view frustrations in the health care experience as inevitable, just part of the package. This is not true. After you've read this book, I'm hoping, you'll look at health care through the eyes of a customer buying a service—and demand alternatives to the elements you hate.

Only markets have the force and tenacity to drive the innovation and efficiency we need. The result will be to bring people together—and in a far more meaningful way than other marketplaces, from coffee shops to retail stores. The intimate, and what physician-author Abraham Verghese calls "sacred," moment of care that takes place during a health exam has been invaded by a Greek chorus of payer requirements and government mandates. It doesn't have to be that way. No one in a free marketplace would ever devise such a system. And I'm convinced that once you and millions of other consumers press for more choices, you will get them. Only then will we have the health care we need and deserve.

PART ONE

My Journey Through
Health Care

CHAPTER ONE

※

The Reason I'm Here

Not long ago, at a gathering in Boston, I had a conversation with an acquaintance who works as a consultant. This guy takes his tennis seriously, and his shoulder was bothering him. He said it was affecting his game. So he was considering an operation that would cost a small fortune. We didn't delve into how he would pay for the surgery, whether his health plan would pick it up, or how much he'd have to kick in. The point was that the functioning of his shoulder mattered greatly to him, and he had the means to fix it, or at least to try.

This conversation took me back to my childhood. I grew up on a genteel, tree-lined street in New York City's Upper East Side. Most summers, we would leave the city for Kennebunkport, in Maine, where my mother and her in-laws would compete with each other to come up with the most beautiful flower beds, the most succulent lobster dinners, or to score a hand-hammered weather vane to give the house the look and feel of Maine. They were trying to out–Martha Stewart each other. Naturally, this included finding the freshest fruit, which led us to a backcountry farm belonging to Betty Gooch. This woman, who seemed ancient to me at the time, raised big fields of berries for a pick-your-own operation. We'd be hunched down picking blueberries, and she'd be nearby, filling pint containers for the tourists too lazy to pick their own. Every so often, she would stand up and give her elbow the most awful whack on a post. When we asked her why, she said, "Well, I got that arthritis and the doctor costs a fortune, but I won't be no left-handed ass-wiper . . . So I just give her a good whack and she'll work again for a couple more hours."

Now you might think that these two scenarios, one featuring the tennis-playing consultant and the other, Betty Gooch, illustrate the unfairness of health care in America. We should have a system, many would argue, that provides Betty with the same expensive surgery should she choose to undergo an operation. Her elbow is worth every bit as much as his shoulder, even if she doesn't use it for a topspin lob. So why should he be back on the court, happily rocketing backhands across the net, while she's stuck slamming her aching elbow into a wooden post?

Let's imagine that we institute a system that guarantees advanced orthopedic surgery for all. It sounds fair and compassionate. In this scheme, the orthopedic practices make money by doing lots of operations and billing as much as permitted for them. While individual consumers don't have to fret about the price, all of us, including Betty, pay for those surgeries with higher premiums and taxes.

If instead we assume the opposite—that none of this surgery is guaranteed—what happens to someone like Betty? First, she presumably pays less for insurance, which puts more money in her pocket. At the same time, orthopedic businesses start looking at her very differently. She's now the prospective customer, a shopper concerned about quality, convenience, and price. They compete for her business, and as they do, they innovate. Prices drop. Maybe Betty opts for similar surgery to the consultant's, or perhaps a simpler and cheaper approach. Or maybe she spends her money on massage, acupuncture, or physical therapy. In any case, she is no longer in a binary market—covered or uninsured, top-line surgery or banging the elbow on a post. She has options. It's up to her. It is this freedom to make choices that will lead to a real health care market, one with many providers, many customers, and many options.

My interest in health care took root early in my life. I wanted a career that would provide the lifestyle I grew up with—the comfortable house, college for kids, the vacations in Maine. But syrupy as this may sound, I also wanted to do good. My family was wealthy and ambitious, but also tied to the principle that we were supposed to serve society. My parents were constantly going to meetings and raising money for social causes. Some of the efforts featured an unlikely mix of privilege and outreach, like my father's attempt to introduce tennis to the poor children of Harlem. But you know what? Lots of kids there actually learned to play and love tennis. It worked.

My uncle George was the model for doing good and doing well. He fought in the Second World War, and then headed to Texas to start his own oil business, Zapata Oil. He did well, sold his share of the business to a partner, and entered public service. He opened up the idea of being a Republican in Texas (That turned out well!), served as ambassador to China, headed the CIA, and eventually rose to the presidency. Should anyone begrudge him his rich man's toy, his high-speed cigarette boat?

When I thought about it, much of my family was settled into politics and finance. My uncle ran for president the year I turned ten. He lost to Ronald Reagan in the primaries and served as Reagan's vice president for the next eight years, and then as the president for the following four. Two of his sons, who later got into politics, were in real estate and oil. But I came from a different branch of the family. My father, also Jonathan, a younger brother of the first President Bush, was the showman of the family. As a student, he sang in the Eisenhower White House as a member of the Yale Whiffenpoofs. Later he was a dancer on Broadway. Eventually he founded an investment management business. But he has always kept a light touch. When his brother was vice president, he would hit up my dad for jokes to tell President Reagan over their weekly breakfast. Some of those jokes would later work their way into Reagan's speeches and interviews. My father encouraged us in everything, but didn't push too hard. The drive came more from my mother, Josephine, who kept the pedal to the metal. So my brother, Billy, and I grew up ambitious, but in a different way from our cousins. He went into a media career, and now has his own radio program and hosts *Access Hollywood*, a syndicated entertainment news show. I angled toward medicine. It seemed like a good choice—at least until I learned that I'd have to ace organic chemistry and molecular biology.

Confronted with that depressing news, I veered toward business. I figured I could blend it with medicine, and end up working in the business of health care. But where was I to start? I had worked on the Bush campaign in 1988, and I got to know the advance teams, the Secret Service, and other people who surrounded my uncle. One of them, Dr. Larry Moore, prepared operating rooms wherever the president or vice president were heading, so that they could be treated quickly in the event of an emergency. A year after the election, when I was looking for a summer job, I buttonholed Larry and asked for career advice. To save lives, he told me, the best plan was to work on an ambulance and get to know a crack trauma unit. The top one, he said, was at Charity Hospital in New Orleans. The leader there was a legendary trauma surgeon named Norman McSwain. His team got lots of practice. The city had the highest rate of gun violence in the country. I soon learned that there were only six ambulances to patrol the city in each twelve-hour shift. That meant that I'd get lots of practice, too.

New Orleans gave me hands-on training in urgent care and, just as important, a primer on American society. This was the 1 percent at the other end. These people were far more isolated and destitute than the poor in New York. The Desire Projects, or Dirty D, were among the worst: desolate cement blocks planted between cypress swamps and the railroad tracks. These neighborhoods were ignored by business, abused by bureaucrats and politicians. They signaled failure at every level—something the rest of the country woke up to fifteen years later while watching the aftermath of Hurricane Katrina.

I got calls into neighborhoods where the only grocery stores were heavily armored vans that pulled up and sold the most miserable food—white bread, Minute rice, Twinkies, hot dogs. They would charge exorbitant prices, taking money through a little slot under the grill, and often squeezing the food out through it. Many of their customers lived in desperate conditions. Some blew up under the pressure. What do you say when a woman throws Drano on a baby, or when a twelve-year-old unloads a Saturday night special on his cousin? You don't say much. You strap the bodies to the stretchers, race back to the ambulance, and gun it to Charity Hospital, the siren screaming.

There was a popular rap song that summer by Public Enemy called "911 Is a Joke." We'd race into LaFitte in the Sixth Ward or Iberville in the Fourth Ward, responding to a stabbing or shooting. It might be midnight, or 1 A.M., and the nine- and ten-year-old kids would be lined up taunting us, "Get up, get down, 911 is a joke in your town!"

It was easy to see why they laughed. We rushed in with the best intentions, and we did save lives. But we didn't change the equation one bit. They had big dysfunctional neighborhoods, where crime was rampant, the schools were backward, and good jobs scarce. Practically the only pathway to advancement was to leave. I certainly wouldn't agree that we were a joke in that town, but we didn't fix the problems. We just hauled away the bodies and patched up the ones we could save.

But it was the contrast between the mean streets of New Orleans and Dr. McSwain's crack trauma unit that got me to thinking about the opportunities for the company I wanted one day to build. In this one nook of the city, Charity Hospital's emergency department, a small cadre of professionals carried out heroic work at a world-class level. Their expertise, however, made a difference only for the most urgent cases. Plenty of other people needed less than Norman McSwain–caliber care. They waited in long lines for medical help, or more often went without it. These people represented a market opportunity. Yes, they were poor, but they generated revenue, either from money they scraped together themselves, or from philanthropy or government aid programs. Someone who came up with a more efficient system for treating them could build a business, and improve their lives.

Naturally, one key for such a company was to hire health care workers who made a lot less money than the doctors on the trauma team. Driving around the city, I saw potential workers everywhere. New Orleans neighborhoods were full of people with no jobs and scant prospects. Each one of those people, as I saw it, was a potential asset, and each noncritical case we hauled in represented an opportunity, a job to do. There was an immense need, and also an immense potential labor force. In the optimal scenario, a company could train and employ the idle workforce to provide needed services in the community. And it could make a profit.

Yes, the workers I'm talking about included people wiping down tables at McDonald's or pumping gas on the access roads to I-10. They might not have a college education. But a number of them could still be trained to take on sophisticated jobs now handled by surgeons or registered nurses, and do it just as well.

I came face-to-face with this unlocked potential in the military. In August 1990, as I was finishing up my summer in New Orleans, the Iraqi army invaded and conquered Kuwait. As I headed back to college at Wesleyan, my uncle George and his team were piecing together a broad international coalition to roll back the Iraqi forces and free Kuwait. This would be known as Operation Desert Storm.

The day after allied bombers launched their first strikes, in January 1991, I enlisted to become a combat medic. In boot camp at Fort Jackson, South Carolina, I met people who had minimal education. One man named Nelson had lived for a year eating from McDonald's and Burger King Dumpsters. He'd been in a youth home, and then kicked out of it. Another, a country kid named Willis, bragged that he could "shoot a tick turd off a deer at two hundred yards." The army had effective programs in place for teaching sophisticated procedures to all of us, no matter what education we came in with. They started with the basics, like pleating pants into tied boots. But within weeks, I could see that Nelson and Willis were operating multimillion-dollar Stinger missile systems. This was some of the most sophisticated equipment for killing people ever devised. But the instructions were broken down into steps that just about anyone could learn: breech locked, scope out and on, back blast area all clear, stay with the target until impact. . . .

Later, when I graduated to medic training, at Fort Sam Houston in

San Antonio, the same model prevailed: Ordinary people were trained to carry out sophisticated work, but now in medicine. Those who tested well were mastering work that in hospitals is entrusted only to surgeons. We were taught to start IVs, to carry out battlefield tracheotomies, and pack grievous wounds. We had sixty guys who could take a soldier who'd been hit by an explosion, put him back together, and get him to safety. Of course, this makes perfect sense. Medics on the scene need to treat wounded soldiers immediately. But wasn't at least part of this scheme applicable to civilian society? If we got this training into the private sector (and loosened up regulations), you'd be getting primary care for $18 an hour.

The first step, as I saw it, is to do what the army does: establish excellent training and protocols, and then triage like crazy. Triage in this case doesn't mean sending someone to a waiting room for three hours. No, it's getting people the care they need, and not have them waiting three hours to see someone with a decade of the world's most advanced and rigorous medical education. Yes, that guy who looks dazed and unsteady should be seen by a doctor, immediately. But many less intense cases can be handled first by well-trained medics. Much of the health care we consume isn't all that complicated. This insight would stick with me.

Well, I never got to Iraq. Desert Storm liberated Kuwait before I shipped out. Reassigned to active reserve, I schlepped back to college and finally wrote that term paper I'd been trying to avoid. I still wasn't much of a student. My mind wandered. But now these mental meanderings had a focus. I wanted to get into the business of medicine. Maybe I would launch a company of my own. If I did, it might feature a few workers with the initial skill sets of Willis and Nelson, and hosts of others below the ranks of doctors and nurses. The trick would be to provide great medical care while deploying fewer highly paid doctors more intelligently. This way, people would pay less and get better service, and I'd make a profit.

That was the dream. But achieving it, I learned as I hunted for my first job, would take some time. I remember having breakfast in New York with Dick Foster, a partner at McKinsey & Company. He was a good friend of the family, well plugged in to business and finance. We met at the restaurant in the Pierre Hotel. Over berries and granola, I told him that I wanted to work in the health care delivery industry, preferably under a CEO who treated patients. He shook his head. "Oh, Jon," he said, "there is no industry for health care delivery." He went on to tell me that I could work for either device manufacturers or a drug company. Pacemakers and pills. That's where the money was in health care. Or maybe I could land a job as a junior administrator at one of the university hospitals. (That was a path, as I saw it, to nowhere.) If I was so inclined, I could labor for some starry-eyed nonprofit and help the world.

In the end I landed a consulting job at Booz Allen. Consulting, I figured, would provide a good look at the options in the industry. So every day I rode the subway from Brooklyn to a big office just a block down from Grand Central Station. Booz had a managed care strategy group that was busy helping regional Blue Cross Blue Shield organizations that had lost their tax-free status, turn into for-profit businesses. They were also working with health maintenance organizations, or HMOs, which were gaining ground at the time. The idea of an HMO—figuring out how to provide services efficiently to a large group of members—wasn't so far from my entrepreneurial dream. Successful HMOs would learn how to optimize precious resources, including doctors' time. I figured I would help them strategize, and learn about the industry in the process.

From day one, however, I knew that I was a misfit in consulting. I didn't have the patience to sit in a swivel chair all day, to pore over health industry studies and come up with reports and recommendations. I couldn't concentrate on it. I couldn't even spell well. Eventually someone would wake up and fire me. In the meantime, I desperately wanted to build something. But this required finding a functioning health care market—or creating one.

This was in 1993, a pivotal year for American health care. In his campaign against my uncle, Bill Clinton had promised a new health plan with insurance for all Americans. As president, he entrusted the job of figuring out how to accomplish this to his wife, Hillary. She and her team put together the Health Security Act. It featured an employer mandate to provide insurance, which they would buy from competitive, but highly regulated, HMOs. Opponents of the bill, including insurance and pharmaceutical companies, sponsored a barrage of advertising, including the so-called Harry and Louise ads. These featured a middle-class couple who were content with the status quo and feared a bill that might force them to settle for plans picked by "government bureaucrats." In one ad, a frustrated Louise lifts a bill from a pile of papers on the kitchen table.

"This was covered under our old plan," she says.

"Yeah, that was a good one, wasn't it?" Harry responds.

"Having choices we don't like is no choice at all," Louise says a few moments later.

"They choose . . . ," Harry says.

"And we lose," his wife finishes the sentence.

The Clinton bill went down in flames, and the fears of Harry and Louise contributed to the Republican takeover of the House of

Representatives in 1994. Over the next few years, health care reform virtually disappeared from the national discussion. The economy was picking up. That reduced anxiety. More important, the rise in health expenditures seemed to be in reverse. In 1993, when Hillary Clinton's commission was putting together its plan, insurance premiums were shooting up 9 percent per year, three times the rate of inflation. By 1995, rates were rising by barely 1 percent. Had the health care industry, which had seemed to be careening out of control, found a way to regulate itself?

In a sense, yes. But it was only temporary. Across the country, scores of HMOs were competing for business. They were doing this in part by offering lower premiums to their corporate customers. Prices fell, at least relative to inflation. The market seemed to be working. There were many HMOs and many shoppers. These customers had choices, and with the recession still fresh in their memories, many of them chose no-frills packages with low premiums for their employees.

From the employee's perspective, paradoxically, the experience felt a bit like Harry and Louise's grim future. They would receive a bill and find that a procedure was no longer covered in their bare-bones plan. Sure, their employers were shopping and saving money, but where was the benefit for the consumer? As the economy motored into the late nineties boom, the press exposed the corporate skinflints who were raking in profits while skimping on coverage. Employees, naturally, pushed for comprehensive health care—the full smorgasbord. Employers, no longer feeling the economic pinch, relented. At the same time, a huge consolidation was taking place among HMOs. The market of many was winnowed down to an oligopoly of a few. Competition withered. Insurance premiums, after a three-year breather, climbed back above inflation.

This was the market I was analyzing as a consultant at Booz Allen. My first project involved Blue Cross Blue Shield of Iowa and South

Dakota. There were studies to read and best practices to consider. As I've mentioned, I was not cut out for this consulting work. That fact became clearer to me by the day. I would take the subway from Brooklyn worrying about a policy white paper I may have overlooked, or a chart with a mislabeled Y-axis. I would gladly have traded that office for a New Orleans ambulance. I would have preferred even boot camp. Why of all places was I stuck in this office? I worried about being fired.

Then one day a new consultant walked in. He was a soft-spoken Korean American named Todd Park. His family, I soon learned, was like a jet propulsion lab for brains. His father, it was said, had more patents at Dow Chemical than anyone except for Mr. Dow himself. While I was a presidential nephew, Todd, as a high school student, was a Presidential Scholar. He went on to Harvard, where he graduated with all the top honors. His younger brother, Ed, was following much the same path.

Todd had focused on health care policy at Harvard. In fact, he wrote his senior thesis on the effect of gatekeepers on HMOs. These were the issues our customers were confronting. What value was there in having a doctor helping to direct coverage for an insurance company? Was it better, for outcomes and the bottom line, to have a highly informed human being making critical decisions about coverage? Or did the human bring emotions and prejudice into a rule-based process that ticked along more efficiently by itself? Of course there were loads of other issues to consider, from staffing to benefits. We traveled all over, to Iowa, to Virginia. We asked questions. We wrote reports. We consulted.

Todd had to be the greatest consultant in the world. He was brilliant. He was focused and organized and meticulous. He put me to shame. I was supposedly his mentor, and I was in line to get fired. My underling was a consulting god.

I did, however, have important lessons to impart. I noticed, for example, that Todd often worked until ten or eleven at night, and then walked down to Park Avenue and waited for the bus. I informed him that consultants who worked late were entitled to call a car service and bill it to the company. For him, this news was as surprising as it was welcome. I also noticed that his clothes were increasingly wrinkled and even a tad dirty. I steered him to a dry cleaner in the neighborhood who could take dirty clothes from our trips in the morning and deliver them pressed and wrapped by the afternoon, again with the company picking up the tab. Todd appreciated this advice.

During those days, I still dreamed of starting my own company. For this, I had a few basic ideas. First, there had to be different markets for different types of customers. One business might help someone like Betty Gooch manage her arthritis, and another highly specialized one could repair the consultant's shoulder. They didn't have to be the same business with the same doctors. That seemed obvious to me. Second, a health care company could train ordinary people, like the ones I'd met in the army, to carry out sophisticated work. A successful start-up would limit the spending on doctors, paying for their precious time and expertise only when no one else could handle the job. Mastering that calculation would be crucial for turning a profit. And then, of course, the start-up would have to be run by the most brilliant, creative, inspired, and industrious team . . .

One day I was ruminating along those lines and wondering for the thousandth time what had led me to become a consultant. I looked over at Todd's desk. There he was, beavering away on one of his flawless business plans. I think it was for Trigon Blue Cross/Blue Shield of Virginia. Then it struck me like a thunderbolt. I had followed this path and come to this job that I sucked at for one simple and compelling reason: to meet Todd Park.

CHAPTER TWO

■

Launching a Starbucks
for Birthing

When I was growing up in Manhattan, I could ride the subway down to Thirty-fourth Street to Macy's. It seemed that I could find just about anything there: feather pillows, Phillips screwdrivers, frying pans, baseball mitts, books, stereos, you name it. Though I didn't know it at the time, the selection at the department store wasn't all that great, and the prices were pretty high. But Macy's was convenient. That was its trump card. You could do all your shopping under one roof.

In the following decades, department stores took a beating as specialist chains emerged. These were category killers. Williams-Sonoma took over the high end of the kitchen. Best Buy cleaned out the home entertainment wing. Containers became an entire market, and a big one. So did olive oil. There was an old cafeteria at Macy's where you could rest for a few minutes on a swivel stool and buy a cup of coffee that tasted like dishwater. Starbucks built a global empire on that meager corner of the market.

Now, of course, we're well into the third stage, which takes place online, or, in today's lingo, in the cloud. These days, a global selection of goods is available at the click of a button, and pricing is utterly transparent. This transforms the marketplace, pushing retailers to offer us even wider selections with greater convenience, all while competing on price. You might argue that much of this is crass materialism, or that we often make stupid spur-of-the-moment purchases. Maybe we do. That's our right. But the marketplace works. It rewards innovators, kills laggards, and provides consumers with better value and more choices.

There are two types of niche businesses that wrest markets from big generalists. One zeroes in on sharply defined segments of customers. An online gourmet cheese shop is an example. So is a boutique bike shop for racers and triathletes. The survival of both businesses hinges on anticipating and fulfilling the needs and appetites of a select group of people. Their mission is to serve and, if possible, delight their customers. Competition forces them to innovate continually. It's why restaurants often change their menus.

The other type of niche operation is the focused factory. To thrive, it must do one narrow job extremely well, more efficiently than its rivals. It masters process. A muffler shop, for example, doesn't have to buy tools and machines to deal with a car's drive train or electrical system. It focuses all of its attention on rusty pipes in the undercarriage. Its workers become experts of that noisy and greasy domain, both because customers demand this mastery and, equally important, because they get loads of practice. Some companies combine both approaches, ruthlessly efficient processes and a focus on precisely what the customer wants. Amazon is an example.

Why am I telling you this? As you may have guessed by now, in the backward and constrained health care economy, the old department store still reigns supreme. It is called the hospital. It attempts to offer every service under one roof. Liposuction, colonoscopies, sprained ankles, C-sections, geriatrics, retina surgery—hospitals do it all. Most of it they carry out with mind-numbing waste and at prices that would horrify (or bankrupt) most of us if we were paying out of pocket. To be fair, many of them are global leaders in their specialties, usually in complex and difficult areas of medicine, such as cancer treatment or liver transplants. But these are small islands in a big and unwieldy pool of . . . everything. Walk into just about any hospital and watch the people wearing hairnets grimly roll gurneys down the corridor. Check out the jammed waiting rooms with the blaring TVs. Is the competitive marketplace anywhere in sight? I don't think so.

Many people go to the hospital for only one test or a single procedure. On these visits, what are the odds that parking will be a headache and service less than charming, that medical records will be missing, that the waiting might take an hour or two, that the procedure will have a glitch, or that the bill will be outrageous? I'd say that chances for at least a couple of those annoyances are extremely high. And each one represents a market opportunity for a focused competitor who can offer that same service with efficiency, convenience, a smile, and better results.

The model for this type of market is LASIK, the popular laser surgery to improve vision. When it was introduced in 1991, LASIK was viewed as risky and expensive. Insurance didn't cover it. LASIK providers operated in office parks and strip malls far from the respectable medical establishment. Some seemed crass. They *advertised*—in the face of strict federal law against it. And many of the early customers suppressed their natural fears and distrust only because they had horrible vision. They were desperate. And many of them got only one eye done. This saved money and hedged against blindness. Since then, the industry has seen steady improvements and innovations. The process is safer, with a 95 percent satisfaction rate. It costs 70 percent less, about $2,000 per eye on average, with some offering rates in the hundreds of dollars. What has fueled its success? The competitive marketplace. Since LASIK surgery is not covered by most insurance plans, people have to compare different services, their satisfaction records, and their prices. In short, they shop around. The industry advances and grows, and hospitals lose a potential growth market.

Hospitals are crammed with other growth markets. Every service they overcharge for and every waiting room full of impatient customers represents a potential opportunity for an entrepreneur. I spent many days and nights twenty years ago mulling the possibilities. With all of the hospitals' inefficiency and hidebound practices, there just had to be an opportunity for me. But which floor of the hospital held the secret? Which services would my company provide?

I was living in Brooklyn at the time with my first wife, Sarah. She was studying to become a nurse. When I would come home, exhausted, after an all-day visit with Todd Park to an HMO in the Badlands or a couple of days on the West Coast, Sarah would educate me in the business of birthing. Hospitals, she said, tended to treat childbirth as a disease. Expectant mothers were processed much like cancer or heart disease patients. They were sent up to rooms on a joyless corridor, with the same hospital smells and carts rolling up and down. Their pregnancy, all too often, was seen as a potential problem, and much of the treatment focused on reducing risk and keeping things on schedule. If labor was going slowly, they often gave the women Pitocin, a drug to strengthen contractions and speed up the process. It could trigger side effects, and produce short and jerky contractions.

If the drug didn't work its magic right away, doctors would often move straight to the caesarian section. The industry, she said, had a natural inclination for C-sections. After all, the procedure bypassed the biological process, with its fits and starts, and put the birth under the science of modern medicine. Doctors dove in and rescued the baby, not only ushering in a new life, but perhaps *saving* two in the process.

From the doctor's perspective, what wasn't to like? Unlike vaginal deliveries, C-sections could be scheduled during the working day, even between rounds of golf. If there were any complications, a doctor who performed a C-section was less likely to face legal challenges. He or she intervened, after all, instead of sitting around and waiting. What's more, women with C-sections spent more days in the hospital, which brought in more revenue.

Sarah compared this to Britain, where midwives handled most of the births. The rate of performing C-sections was dramatically lower there, and the results were better. Just as important, she said, midwives focused more on the mother's needs and comforts, and they celebrated birth as a flowering of human health. It was anything but a disease.

I started to think about midwives. They were an example of what I'd been looking for since my days in New Orleans and in the army. Like army medics, they had training for specific jobs, and could do highly sophisticated work—but at a pay level far below that of surgeons. I looked into the numbers. Insurance companies reimbursed hospitals an average of $15,000 for each birth. (By 2010, the average price for vaginal deliveries was up to $30,000, and for C-sections $50,000, with insurance companies reimbursing an average of $18,329 and $27,866 respectively.) Midwives in the nineties made between $50,000 and $75,000 a year, one quarter as much as physicians. Only one of ten births required a doctor. If midwives could handle 85 or 90 percent of the births, then we'd need far fewer expensive MDs. A Dartmouth study indicated that best practices, including the broader use of midwives, could reduce the cost of birthing by 20 percent. If we delivered babies for $3,000 less, then we could conceivably split the savings with insurance companies. Four million babies were born every year in the United States, each representing a potential profit of $1,500. Multiplying those numbers came to a tantalizing $6 billion. We figured we could double the revenue per birth of the medical practice, with only a 15 percent increase in cost for staffing, management, and information systems.

A new approach to birthing could be built on the focused factory model. Women, after all, put a lot of thought and study into choosing a gynecologist or obstetrician. This was one lonely outpost of the industry where shopping actually occurred. And shopping gave new competitors a chance. My company, hopefully, could provide the new mothers with a warm and supportive environment, personal attention, better care, and superior results. Behind the scenes, we would run a ruthlessly efficient operation, with a laser focus on costs.

I considered Starbucks. At that time, Starbucks's CEO, Howard Schultz, was creating a market around a pseudo-Italian product with a feeling of community and tattooed baristas who learned customers' names and could discuss Walt Whitman or mushroom risotto or last night's Cubs game. Behind all the banter and gab, Schultz instituted standardized practices and cost control with the zeal and discipline of a highly caffeinated Henry Ford—all while charging $4 for a latte. If Schultz could build an empire around the latte, why couldn't we pull off the same trick with birthing? Yes, we would be the Starbucks of obstetrics, a no-nonsense moneymaker that's warm on the outside and knows the customers' needs, tastes, and phobias. Word of mouth would drive business our way. We would start in one city, learn the ropes, and then expand. I began to get very excited. On our trips, Todd and I discussed the birthing business endlessly. It seemed like a golden opportunity.

It was around then that I got a letter in the mail. It was from Harvard Business School and addressed to midcareer professionals. The school offered an eighteen-month MBA program. Better yet, applicants didn't have to take the standardized tests, the GMATs. As I've mentioned, I was never an exemplary student and certainly didn't consider myself a likely Harvard candidate. I did, however, have the seed of a true birthing business sprouting in my head. If I managed to get into B-school, I wouldn't just be getting a prestigious diploma. Instead, I'd be harnessing the school and its professors behind my start-up idea. At the same time, admission to Harvard would provide a graceful and timely exit from the consulting job.

So I applied. I poured into the application my excitement about the start-up idea, and the broader concept of bringing the discipline of business into health care. I had Sarah comb through the application and fix all the spelling mistakes and sentence fragments. There was a form on the application where you had to affirm that no one helped with it. I wrote a note explaining that Sarah had helped, and if that was a problem, well, they'd have to reject me. Instead, they accepted me.

I moved to Cambridge. For the first time in my life, I was an inspired student. In fact, I was a zealot. I wanted to start a company, and practically everything I could learn at Harvard was relevant. Many of my classmates looked at finance courses or management seminars as résumé items, skills that prospective employers might care about. I, by contrast, was plugging the lessons straight into my birthing company, which I was sure would be hiring workers, managing them, billing customers, and delivering babies within months. I needed to know this stuff.

In the spring semester, there was a business plan competition at the school. The winners would get some funding. I submitted my plan for the birthing business, and I had every reason to expect to finish near the top. After all, mine wasn't just some idea dreamed up for the contest. It was a true opportunity, backed up by serious market research and a business plan that real investors would be rifling through within months.

Imagine my surprise and outrage when my plan didn't even make the first cut. Was it something they failed to understand? Had I left out the financing or confused the numbers? I went to Joe Lassiter, the professor who headed up the contest, and I asked him. Using a baseball analogy, he explained that he and his team were looking for risky home runs or sure-thing doubles. In other words, if a business plan was iffy, it had to have a stupendous upside. Otherwise, it should be a safe bet. "Yours," Lassiter told me, "is a risky double."

The risks were easy enough to understand. My company was in health care, after all, an industry that's hostile to start-ups. You have to deal with prickly doctors, regulations galore, malpractice suits, and you have to figure out how to get paid by a confusing web of insurers, private and government alike, who are experts at finding reasons not to pay. What's more, he said, the birthing business doesn't scale easily. Unlike a software start-up, where a single application can sell by the millions, a birthing business would require difficult rollouts in every region. In short, a risky double.

He made good points, but every obstacle could be overcome with endless work and fabulous execution. He didn't understand how great we were going to be. I had leadership skills that were not evident in the business plan. And I was going to start this business with Todd Park, probably the best co-founder a start-up could have. The professor had never met Todd. He had no idea.

Spring break in Cambridge is a bit of a misnomer. The snow is still around, but just slushier. Wind whips through the bare branches in Harvard Yard. Most of my classmates headed off for R & R in the sun. But I made photocopies of my business plan and flew to the annual conference of the American College of Obstetricians and Gynecologists in Las Vegas. I attended seminars on the risks and rewards of episiotomies (high risk, low reward), low-dose aspirin therapy to prevent preeclampsia, issues involved in vaginal births following C-sections, changes in Medicare funding. That was all very interesting, of course, but the real purpose of my visit was to find doctors who would team up with my still unnamed company. I needed partners.

These people had to understand and appreciate a business that would zero in on what I call the "soft profit belly" of birthing. Just about every successful business on earth has some area in which it makes easy money. This is usually where it benefits from an inefficiency. Maybe the customer doesn't have all the facts, or is unable, for one reason or another, to move to a competing provider. Maybe a state law keeps competitors out. These profit bellies are wonderful while they last. Department stores like Macy's thrived for decades selling slightly overpriced goods to people who didn't want to lug all their bags out into the street and shop for better bargains at Sears, Bloomingdales, or on Canal Street.

In a functioning market, these soft profit bellies attract competitors. They see the money, and they know they can grab a slug of it if they address the inefficiency, reduce the friction, or enhance the experience. Specialty stores and, later, online retailers grew off the profit bellies of department stores.

In the business Todd and I were hatching, the profit belly was in the hospital. It was inefficient beyond belief. But because it operated in a market without shoppers, it was able to overcharge. This provided a comfortable and prosperous life for thousands upon thousands of ob-gyn doctors. Our challenge was to find doctors among them who were ready to attack their own industry, to replace many of their kind with cheaper and more efficient midwives. Instead of skimming profits from a wasteful operation, they would help us pioneer an efficient one and make money from the savings. At the same time, by delegating more routine births to the midwives, doctors could focus on the more complicated cases where their skills were needed. Despite this compelling logic, it was not an easy sell.

But in the convention at Las Vegas, I found a taker. His name was Mitch Besser. He was a passionate obstetrician. In a federally funded trial, he and his colleagues in San Diego had just been implementing a plan resembling ours—more midwives, more focus on the mother, best practices driven by statistics. The results looked promising. But the hospital wasn't cooperating. They wouldn't even let midwives into their tertiary care units. It was pretty clear to Mitch and his partners that implementing this different business model within the hospital was going to meet even more resistance. So they wanted to divorce the hospital and start their own birthing business. For this, they needed a well-funded partner. This was our chance.

Even before business school ended, Todd and I were starting up the company. Todd quit his job at Booz Allen and moved to Boston. We set up corporate headquarters in the basement of my house in Lincoln. I hit up family and friends for funding and gathered $1.4 million for what would become Athena Women's Health.

Early that summer, we brought the president of Mitch's San Diego group, Bill Schwartz to Boston. I recruited six employees so that we looked bigger and more established than we were. Our new chief technology officer, Bob Gatewood, didn't know anything yet about health care. But he had a degree in *rocket science*. That had to impress. We didn't show Schwartz the basement in Lincoln, with the desks made from old doors on sawhorses and cables snaking through the room. We met in conference rooms in Boston, where we outlined our business plan with all of the assurance of Booz Allen consultants. We showed him the numbers. We took him to a Red Sox game. At the end of the visit, we were all in the car, Todd, my brother Billy and I, and Bill Schwartz. We still didn't know what he thought. As we pulled up to his hotel, he told us that he was "very impressed by what he'd seen, and that we should 'do something.'"

We climbed out of the car, said good-bye. When we got back in the car, Todd said, "I'm overwhelmingly euphorically ecstatic. But I'm not going to react because he can still see us . . ."

We bought the San Diego practice from Bill and Mitch's group of doctors. Their team would continue to work for the new company. By the time we set out for California, in the fall of 1997, there were four of us in the management group, all guys in our twenties. It was a bit strange, we knew, for young men to launch a birthing start-up. But people in their twenties have an enormous advantage when it comes to outsized challenges. They have less experience whispering in their ear about how risky and stupid the venture is. Further, young people generally have much less to lose. And they have incredible energy. So with this mixture of energy, ignorance, and confidence bordering on insanity, we set out to revolutionize childbirth in America.

Our new company started out with twelve clinics scattered through San Diego County. The six doctors and thirty-five midwives were doing two thousand births a year. The midwives were all Latinas. They were warm and friendly and supportive, just what our business plan called for. We quickly began decking out the birthing centers with features that would appeal to the mothers. Warm colors, natural fibers, sunlight, tubs for those who wanted to have their babies in water. The comfort of the mother and the baby was a top priority.

Early on, I flew one weekend from San Diego to a wedding in Albuquerque. A friend told me to look up Leslie Brunner, who was working in integrated delivery at Lovelace Clinic and writing a paper on the collaborative approach to childbirth. Here's what she has to say about the impression I was making during the early start-up phase of our new company:

I'd told Jonathan to meet me in delivery. I see this guy coming down the hall with a stroller. He was talking loudly on a giant phone with a huge antenna. Back then, people were very cautious about using phones in hospitals, but he wasn't. He had a pager about twice the size of a billfold clipped to his belt. He had so much energy that I remember thinking of Tasmanian Devils.

I told him what we were doing in labor and delivery. In Albuquerque, two thirds of the population is Native American and Hispanic. Many of them are distrustful of doctors, and they like midwives. So we were trying to prove the model.

We went to the cafeteria, Jonathan and I and his daughter, Nicola, who was in the stroller. By this point, I'd probably known him for thirty minutes. He started talking to me about starting this company. He was spitting food as he talked. Then he started eating off my plate. (I'm from the South, and you don't do that.) He was so excited, and I thought, This is what I'm missing. The fact is, I was working in this great clinical environment, but there was no creativity or spark.

Before he left, he said he was starting this company, and that I had to go work there. The trouble was, I'd worked at Lovelace for only a couple of months, and I wasn't really sure that his company existed yet. I said, "Good luck, sounds kind of risky and you're kind of crazy. So good-bye."

I must have done something right, because eight months later, Leslie quit her job in New Mexico and came to Athena Women's Health in San Diego. Her assignment was to rescue our troubled company.

CHAPTER THREE

The Pivot

We landed in San Diego in the fall of 1997 brimming with confidence, ready to take over our newly acquired birthing centers and pioneer a new chapter in women's health. If our plan was a dream, San Diego seemed custom-made for it. The whole place had an otherworldly vibe. The parks were soft and green, with grass groomed like golf courses. These were nothing like the playgrounds of my Manhattan Upper East Side childhood, where the ground was hard dirt that smelled of pee. The Mexican food was outstanding. And though it didn't make much difference to us at the time, San Diego was pioneering something very few people had even heard of then: the broadband Internet. Eventually, this would become important to our business.

We rented a crash pad for the whole management team in the Hillcrest neighborhood, just around the corner from the Scripps Mercy Hospital. We dropped mattresses in the bedrooms and set up offices downstairs. Then we launched our business of bringing babies into the world—in a safer, cheaper, friendlier, and more profitable way. The doctors, who had sold us the practice, were on board with the business model. They would treat fewer patients, but would supervise an efficient system that would handle more of them. We would combine the lowest cost and highest quality, producing the happiest mothers and healthiest babies. We'd all make money. Just nail it in San Diego, we figured, then raise more venture funding and take the business national.

It was at this early stage, however, that I came to grips with one reason that so many people had been steering me away from a heath care start-up: It's ridiculously hard to get paid. Sure, kitchen contractors or educational consultants deal with deadbeats and delays, and have to send out invoices time and again. But health care payments occupy their own circle of hell. There are different forms to fill out, cryptic codes to apply, and confounding eligibility requirements, and if one tiny detail isn't exactly right, instead of getting paid, the form comes back . . . and you try again. For incumbents, a complicated and arcane system provides an effective defense. While insiders master it, new challengers struggle, and even starve. And starving competitors are the best kind, at least for the short time they're around.

The birthing business had its own special challenges. We opened up a file for each woman who came to us, and we carefully noted each visit and each expense. But we couldn't bill for our work until the baby was born, seven or eight months later. Even that payment was often delayed or rejected, for one reason or another, or else disappeared into the ether and had to be tracked down. Of course, not all of the pregnancies resulted in a birth. For miscarriages and other misfortunes, we had to go back and bill for the work we put in. This was a time drain. And meanwhile, we were busy fighting other obstacles the incumbents threw into our path. Hospitals, citing a shortage of qualifications, wouldn't permit our midwives into their delivery rooms.

Just as bad as the payment struggle was the information fog: We simply could not see what was happening in our business. We had little idea of how much money we were losing, or how much we were owed. The facts, if you could call them that, were floating around on pieces of paper, and in computer systems we didn't control. Even today, with the growth of electronic health records, the industry is still immersed in fog. Invoices go on for pages, written in codes that only the initiated understand. Many proprietary computer systems don't talk to each other. And the dollar numbers on bills often represent an aspirational number for a hospital or clinic. For example, in the best of cases, a payer might reimburse $18,000 for a colonoscopy, though the final negotiated number may turn out to be one-tenth that amount—once the tedious back-and-forth, often including faxes and mail, is concluded. The result is confusion, uncertainty, and fog.

This is bad for newcomers, and also for innovation. Think about it. For an industry to generate new ideas and procedures, companies need both the freedom to make changes, and also the ability to see what effect they have. Every business is a laboratory, and requires feedback. Software start-ups on the Internet are a shining example. They launch their services on Apple's app store or Android, or they hitch up with PayPal, and if they catch on, money literally flows into their accounts. They have automatic billing—no invoices, no permissions, eligibility requirements, authorizations, co-pays, no faxes or snail mail, in short, no nightmare. But equally important, they can follow what's working and what's not, and make fixes. They literally see what they're doing. And what happens? Hundreds of thousands of entrepreneurs flock to the industry. They innovate and grow.

It didn't occur to me until later, much later, that solving the misery of payment and clearing the fog had the potential to become even a bigger business than a nationwide network of birthing clinics. But it's awfully hard to imagine solving a problem for everyone else, when that very problem appears utterly mystifying (and is in the process of grounding your business into fine and pungent dust).

We should have known to expect more troubles. The doctors who sold us the practice had many of the same ones, including the challenge of getting paid. And one of the last things they did, before handing us the keys, was to sign a five-year deal with a medical billing service way up in Encinitas run by a guy named Rich Maiatico. They probably thought they were doing us a favor. But it was one of the nastiest of the many surprises I came upon in those early days.

While getting paid was critical, understanding the process was equally important. The data held the secrets to our business. Yet instead of processing it ourselves, we handed our paperwork, all of the forms and the doctors' scribblings, to a guy who pulled by the offices every day. He'd transport this intelligence north, through twenty-five miles of freeway hell, to Maiatico's office. There they had a software system called "Medical Manager." Someone would type all the data from our papers into the system. Then their modem would dial onto the network and submit the claims.

We had no information at all. At the fifteenth of every month, we would receive a box full of green reports from the billing service up in Encinitas, each one fourteen inches wide. And that would tell us what we did the previous month. It detailed the cash that came in, but because the payments were so uneven and different, it was impossible to tell what our revenues really were on any given month until three or four months later.

"We know last month sucked!" we'd say to Maiatico. "Tell us what's happening now!" But of course he had no data on hand.

What's worse, we were only getting paid on about 65 percent of the claims we were submitting. The other 35 percent, we learned on our frequent trips up to Encinitas, were problematic. Something was wrong, some detail was missing, or some new mother in our clinic was ineligible for insurance. We were missing out on more than one third of our revenue, and we usually didn't know why. The most fundamental data point of our business—the bottom line—was a mystery to us. Uncovering it required more research.

Getting to the bottom of it was up to Bob Gatewood. Like me, Bob was in his late twenties. He was an aerospace engineer, and was especially interested in developing software. Early on, my cofounder Todd and I told him that we needed a chief technology officer. Bob said he didn't see why we'd need one for a birthing business. But we explained that to run the business the efficient way we anticipated, we'd need a nationwide billing system. That made his ears perk up a bit.

Our talk with Bob occurred in the summer of 1997, months before we plunged into our San Diego adventure. We were still operating in the trashed-out basement of my house in Lincoln, Massachusetts. It had phones and papers strewn around, and big pipes wrapped in what looked like vintage asbestos. We had a computer set up on a table between two card tables. My wife and I had just had our second baby, whose gurgling and cries upstairs added to the ambient noise. And whenever things got slow, it seemed, our eternally hungry cat, Compass, would drag in a dying mouse or flapping bird. Athena Women's Health did not look like a corporation beelining to the top. But that was part of its charm. When Bob learned about our big plans and the venture money we were raising, and when he sensed how excited we were about the new business, he signed on.

The first order of business for the new CTO was to buy billing software. So Bob brought in Todd's younger brother, Eddie, and his roommate from college, Justin. Eddie had just graduated from Harvard and would be going to work that September at a consultancy in the white-hot Internet business. Bob and Eddie started calling up big software companies. Athena, they told them, was setting up a nationwide chain of women's health centers, and would be requiring the appropriate software. To the software vendors, this sounded like a mouthwatering

contract. They hurried to book meetings at this new company's corporate offices, at 94 Codman Road, in Lincoln. The house lay along a
section of rural road that passed through forest. It looked like one of the
lonelier stretches Paul Revere must have galloped along on his famous
ride. Our house sat back from the road, camouflaged by trees. We
would watch the confounded sales reps driving slowly back and forth
before parking and venturing tentatively up the driveway, decked out
in their corporate suits, convinced that they somehow had the wrong
address. I remember one woman approaching cautiously, as if she had
encountered a rural meth lab, and then snapping off her heel on the
loose driveway gravel.

They were a little taken aback by our shabby basement "headquarters," and usually surprised—sometimes just amused—to find a group
of twenty-something *men* embarked on a women's-health start-up. All of
the software systems these people were selling cost way too much. Not
one was built for doctors or for the Internet. They weren't right for us.

It was several months later, after starting up in San Diego, that we
saw what a waste it would have been to invest in advanced software.
Health care—the entire industry—still ran on paper, reams and reams
of it. The company we took over came with only four computers, none
of them linked to a network. Software would have provided little more
than forms to print out. (In other words, it meant just a slight step up
from doctors' offices in 2014 that continue, against all logic, to hand
patients clipboards and pens.) Communication among our San Diego
offices involved typing memos and faxing them to the twelve offices. If
you wanted to contact someone quickly, you dialed a pager. So Bob's
technical job started out on the most primitive level. His first order of
business as chief technology officer was to install group voice mail.
That advanced our communications exponentially.

As the payment problems began to mount, Bob would drive the most impossibly tiny rental car, a Chevy, up to Encinitas to see Maiatico. He had to find out what was happening up there. We were sending off one set of numbers, and the ones coming back were different, as if they weren't even from the same business. Every time we ran a spreadsheet, we came up with different results. It was as if we were running our company blind. Bob would sit down next to Adelle, the systems administrator, and say, "Hey, can you run this report? How many claims did we do yesterday? Why did these ones fall into a black hole?"

Then Bob would ask about exceptions, and different billing protocols. Sometimes I joined him. We were just trying, desperately, to figure it all out. In the process, we were driving Rich and Adelle crazy. I'm sure they groaned every time that Chevy pulled up in the parking lot.

It dawned on us fairly soon that we weren't unique by any stretch. Struggling medical businesses around the country were suffering with their own versions of Maiatico. If we were different from the rest, maybe we were more zealous about our business, scared to be running out of venture funding, freaked out over impending death. Since our whole business was tied up in the payments mess, we tended to fixate on that.

One day, Bob came up with a simple truth: Some people knew how to get paid. Most doctors certainly weren't poor. That meant that the secret wasn't to be found at Maiatico's in Encinitas, where no one had the answer. The people who had the system figured out worked elsewhere: at successful medical practices. Bob started to invite himself to these companies, camping out in the payments division, waiting for his chance to ask questions.

This was where he came face-to-face with Gladys. Let me describe her for you. She's about fifty-eight years old, a sharp and no-nonsense sort. Type A. She's often angry. She hates insurance companies with a passion. She climbed to her current rank though a decades-long slog of apprentice jobs. She scurried to find numbers and matching claims to satisfy the know-it-all task mistresses who once ordered her around. Now she's in charge. Gladys is an oracle of insurance payment minutiae and she tends to bark out her knowledge to her subordinates—the frontline troops. "That policy pays for a gynecological visit once every eighteen months . . ." Each one of these underlings should know all of these facts—but doesn't yet. So Gladys puts herself into the middle of the information flow. She's essential. If someone forgets to check eligibility or if a piece of code is missing, the claim doesn't get paid. Gladys makes sure it will. Every day Gladys looks at all of the payments, and all of the rejections, the denied claims. She organizes them by dollar amount, with the biggest on top, and then figures out who screwed up. She sits for hours on the phone with insurance companies, arguing loudly.

Gladys was not, in fact, an actual person. She was our name for a specific type of person. But Bob found one version of her or another in every successful medical practice he visited. He got to know Gladys. He understood her function. Gladys knew the rules.

On his visits, Bob noticed something peculiar about Gladys's frontline troops: They would all plaster every square inch of free space on their weighty computer monitors with Post-it notes, each one with a different exception. Something to remember about one insurance company, one ailment, or one type of claim.

Bob's original mission at the company was to manage software. Faced with what he was learning about Gladys, the solution seemed self-evident. He simply had to code every single rule that Gladys knew, every one of those Post-it notes, into a software program. The computer would master the rules better than any human. It would be faster and more thorough than even the queen of all the Gladyses. Computer programs certainly had their shortcomings. They struggled with situational context and they mangled human language. But if there was one thing they mastered, it was rules. If we were ever going to grow beyond San Diego, or even survive there, Bob needed the right computer program, a digital Gladys.

That's what he told me. It was a misty spring day. We were standing in the lobby of our office. Babies were busy being born upstairs. If you looked in the door, you might think we had a booming business. Births were up 50 percent. But with little idea about the revenue coming our way, it felt like we were going broke. The question was whether it made sense for a struggling women's health care company to take on a major software project. Everything I'd learned at business school, and in life, said no. A company should focus on its core competence, what it's really good at, and stay clear of businesses it doesn't know.

It turned out that Bob had heard about a small company nearby that was building something very close to what we were looking for, a rules engine that could handle medical billing. It wouldn't be our program. But maybe if we paid them a bit of money and lent them a programmer—like Todd's brother, Eddie—we could populate the program with all of the relevant rules we needed, and then license the system for free. We would have our digital Gladys.

That was the deal we cut. Eddie, following his summer stint with us, had gone on to work at Viant, one of the early Internet consultancies. They were helping traditional companies, like Sears or Chrysler, figure out this brand-new medium, the Internet. This was the dot-com boom, a time of excitement and insanity. The Fed chairman, Alan Greenspan, had recently warned of "irrational exuberance" in the markets. Lots of stupid stuff was happening, and Internet companies with no revenue were soaring on the stock market. At the same time, though, established companies really did have to start figuring out how they would operate in a world of e-commerce and ubiquitous information. Eddie, working in New York City, was helping them. But when he got a fairly urgent call from his brother, he took a leave from Viant, threw a suitcase in his Camry, and drove from New York to San Diego. "My brother needed me more," he later said.

Now Todd Park is a classic first son. He and his brother grew up in Ohio, the sons of Korean immigrants, and while the boys were starring in school their father was filing a dizzying string of patents at Dow Chemical. Todd was eager to please, which in that family meant learning, climbing, and excelling. Even today, as President Obama's chief technology officer for the U.S. Government, he takes on every assignment—even the crashing debut of the federal health care Web site—as a problem waiting to be fixed. He's eternally optimistic. And when he puts his big mind and all of his energy behind a project, he has reason to be. Not long ago, he came back from Italy with a gift for me, a little pewter container engraved with the words *Tutto e Possibile*, or Everything Is Possible. That's not something I'd ever buy, but it's pure Todd. Eddie, the second child, is equally skilled, but has a different personality. I consider him the Grim Enabler.

When Eddie reached San Diego, he lugged a thirty pound computer tower up the stairs and set it up next to his mattress. Then he holed himself up in that room and banged away, coding. He didn't know anything about health care. So Bob would spend a lot of time in there with him, telling him what he was culling from the Gladyses of the world. It wasn't too long before it dawned on us that the only person doing any programming on this project was Eddie. In essence, we were paying the other company for a program that our employee was creating. So we split from them. Eddie started coding the program from scratch, this time using the open-source Linux operating system. In his mind, he was building a universal system, one for which programmers around the world could build applications. It would work on the Web, and on everyone's computer. We still thought Eddie was building a tool just for us. But even in those early days, I think he knew that he was building a global medical records program. At Viant, he had been busy working on e-commerce and e-strategies. Now he was creating the same thing for Athena.

Todd and I, meanwhile, were busy dealing with another problem altogether: The better our company got at our mission—delivering healthy babies efficiently in a warm and supportive environment—the more trouble we ran into. We were becoming what's known as a "shit magnet." I'll explain.

Our service was getting very good. Our costs were low, our midwives and doctors expert. And our best practices led to far more healthy and natural pregnancies and far fewer trips to the intensive care unit. Only 10 percent of our births were delivered by C-section, about one-third of the national average. Ninety percent of the mothers who gave birth in our centers breast-fed their babies, compared to the 67 percent national average at the time. (Now it's close to 80 percent.) We avoided the common widening incisions called episiotomies, which are expensive, horribly uncomfortable for the mother, and statistically counterproductive. Our centers were delivering healthy babies and were filled, for the most part, with joy. This combination made for happier customers and lower costs.

Our growing popularity led pregnant women across the San Diego area to us. They began to switch insurance carriers to ones that covered births at Athena. Many would have their babies in one of our centers and then return to their previous physicians. After all, they often didn't want to change their family doctor or pediatrician or dental plan. They simply wanted to shop for the right place to have a baby. And they couldn't shop without jumping from one insurance carrier to another.

Our popularity worked against us. It was the opposite of the way a sane market operates. Because we were popular, we attracted customers for what to most women is the most expensive medical procedure of their pre-Medicare years. Increasingly, health plans that offered Athena would receive three or four months of premiums and then pay claims that averaged $12,000—and then lose the customer. The insurers began to view us as toxic. A shit magnet. Growing numbers of health plans fired us by kicking us out of their networks.

Pretty soon, most of our remaining clients were indigent. They were either on Medicaid, or they had no insurance at all and paid in cash. Or promised to pay in cash . . . Here we were, the largest obstetric practice in San Diego County, and our business was mostly Medi-Cal, the state welfare program, and migrant workers. We needed their business, and even appealed to them with Spanish-language ads on local TV.

"All migrants all the time." It was a laugh line for us, but not a very funny one. This was not the thriving business we envisioned. We were hemorrhaging money.

Now think about what was happening to us, and how it reflects a health care system that was—*and continues to be*—seriously misaligned. We were offering a service that delivered superior results and was cheaper. Customers switched health plans to deliver their babies in our centers. They tried to shop! But their shopping created problems for insurers, who then removed our cheaper and more popular offering from their plans. Is that the way markets are supposed to work? In the end, the only people we could attract were those who were outside the system, women who scraped together money and shopped for value.

You're probably wondering if the market has grown more sensible since the late nineties. The answer is no. A study by Castlight Health, a data company co-founded by Todd Park in 2008, recently compared cost and quality of births in major U.S. cities. The most expensive births, in New York, Chicago, and Seattle, also ranked as the lowest in quality (as measured by incidence of jaundice among newborns and the rate of deliveries before full term). In Chicago, the gap between price and quality is the most striking. At one hospital with above-average results, the average price for a normal pregnancy and delivery costs $5,325. For the same service, a nearby hospital with below-average scores charges $17,000.

We were clearly on the losing side of the equation. Still, we struggled to rescue the company. Todd, especially, was working like a madman. He was scheduling meetings with doctors at two in the morning, or three, when they came off shift. He wasn't eating well. He wasn't sleeping. He crashed rental cars. One time he ran out of gas in the middle of Interstate 10, at rush hour. He'd forgotten to look at the gauge.

Part of the problem was data. Our business plan was built upon demonstrating to insurance companies that we saved them money, and splitting the savings. We were generating an average of $1,500 of savings per birth, but didn't have the data to prove it. They'd say, "We believe that the births you're doing are a subset that are inexpensive." It seemed clear to them. How else to explain that only 10 percent of our customers were getting C-sections? We replied that our superior process reduced the number of C-sections, which were often unnecessary (and worse for the mothers). This fell on deaf ears. They kept meeting with us, saying that they wanted to identify the savings we'd created. But how do you identify the cost of a C-section that doesn't take place? Should we start sending our customers to intensive care just to teach the insurance carriers a lesson? What we needed was to show, step-by-step, our state-of-the-art process. But for that we needed data.

While these struggles continued in San Diego, I was convinced that the only way to save the company was to expand it. I was flying around, negotiating with practices in Rhode Island and Connecticut. Maybe, I thought, our model would work better in one of those markets. Maybe we wouldn't be a shit magnet. Maybe we'd make money. Of course, when I called venture funds and said I was looking for a new infusion, they saw what business I was in and ran away from me, hair on fire.

While Todd and I were killing ourselves to save the business, Leslie Brunner had finally quit her job in New Mexico to join us. We sent her to San Diego. Maybe she could squeeze out some savings, we thought, though we suspected that the problems were too deep and serious for one manager to fix. While the birthing businesses tanked, Eddie and Bob stayed holed up in that room with the mattress and the computer. I grew to resent them. They insisted they were making progress, but as far as I could see, they were shutting themselves off from our increasingly dire problems, and were just geeking out with the computer. The program, their digital Gladys, seemed like their toy. Tensions were high. Increasingly, we barked at each other.

Then one day Eddie and Bob showed me a surprising feature of their new system. Eddie had programmed in an application that combed through California's online database to check the insurance eligibility of each potential customer. Checking for eligibility was tedious work that humans performed slowly and miserably, and at great cost. It required endless phone calls and digging through files looking for this vital detail. And often the humans got it wrong, which meant that we didn't get paid—at least not quickly, and not enough. Now, though, this evolving digital Gladys could handle it. This was like elixir. Maybe, I thought, Bob and Eddie were on to something.

They kept working. Todd continued laboring into a near catatonic state. At one point, he was strung out from lack of sleep, and felt despair. He started to cry and said he wanted to quit. My response was different. I was getting meaner and angrier, trying to beat my way to victory. "You can't quit," I said. "I went to everyone I've met since I was sixteen years old to fund this thing, and we can't let it collapse."

I reached the conclusion not long ago that anger, either white hot or smoldering, is a fundamental fuel for entrepreneurs. They don't have to be angry all of the time, of course; that would be no fun for anyone. But it helps if deep down they nurse some wound, grievance, or perhaps a sense of injustice. The anger gets them stoked. I think Steve Jobs was often angry. I often see myself as friendly and humorous. Sometimes I am, but in thinking through phases of my life for this book, I realized that during many of my most productive stretches, I was seething, and also terrified of impending failure. This combination of fear and anger, along with a good bit of luck, served me well during those difficult months.

In the end, Todd didn't quit. That was just a moment of self-pity. But around that time, he and his wife took a short vacation to Paris. From what I heard, they just slept. Meanwhile, I continued hunting down money. Venture funders tried their best to avoid me. Of course, I wasn't dumb. This was the dot-com bubble, and we had an Internet feature. So I began to market the company's state-of-the-art Web-based billing system. This was one of its prime assets, along with low costs, fewer C-sections, and healthy babies. With time (and out of desperation), I started to work more of the technology component into my standard spiel. This led a few bankers to take my calls. They would express initial interest. Then, puzzled, they'd ask about Athena's 105 employees. What were all these people doing? Well, I started to explain, some were doctors, others were midwives, others. . . . At this point, they ran away screaming.

Turns out that when you're trying to raise money for a sinking business, word gets out. People don't take your calls. And the only ones who do are either hopelessly out of the loop, or they see something in the business that others are missing. Of course, the message you give them is that you're extremely busy—completely overwhelmed with calls—but maybe you can squeeze them into the schedule somewhere.

That was the message I gave to a venture funder from Dallas in March 1998. His name was Mark Wilson, from Stone Capital. He was coming to San Diego to meet me. I knew at the time that this might be our last chance to land a financial lifeline for Athena. I was thinking, or hoping, that he believed he was in a crowd of eager investors. But by that point it was a crowd of one. We tidied up the office at our main birthing center, made sure that it was fully booked, buzzing with efficient staffers and knowledgeable midwives, all of them fully engaged in the extremely lucrative business of bringing healthy babies into the world.

We put Wilson in the lounge behind birth room 5, where he had a chance to sit down and take in the scene, and I launched into my P. T. Barnum pitch about the bright future for Athena Women's Health, a focused factory for health care, the Starbucks of birthing.

He cut me off with a wave of his hand. "I'm not interested in your birthing business," he said flatly. "But I can get you eleven million dollars for rights to your software."

Silly me, I turned down that offer. I was still committed to reinventing the birthing business. But it didn't take me long to see the light.

Within weeks, we pivoted to our new business: data. It wasn't going to be an easy transition. The birthing business had to die. Our wonderful doctors and midwives would work for someone else. I remember wrenching meetings where we all drank too much and practically everyone cried. But there was a soaring logic to this transition. First, we were no longer going to stay up all night and argue with gynecologists. Other companies could do that. We had built a system to handle the administrative chores that the vast majority of doctors hated—and sucked at. If our machines could handle this work for them, they'd be free to do what they loved. Doctors would take care of patients. And we would grow the business to new levels.

That was my new pitch to investors, and believe me, they took my calls. It was 1999, the height of the dot-com boom, and the new athenahealth was reborn as an Internet company.

CHAPTER FOUR

Government (or, How My Cousin, the President, Almost Killed My Company)

By the time summer 2004 rolled around, it had been five years since we exited the San Diego birthing business. We stopped hiring midwives and started recruiting software engineers. We were an Internet business, and those investors who used to run away screaming at the very mention of my name promptly rushed back with fists full of dollars. The dot-com bust came a year later. But it was barely a speed bump for the new athenahealth. That same year my cousin George was elected president. He was a funny, charismatic figure from my youth, but I hadn't seen much of him since.

I was now the CEO of a rising medical data company. We built automated systems to handle the administrative chores for thousands of medical practices. They didn't buy anything from us. Instead, they subscribed to a service on the Internet. This was what would later be called a cloud-based service, but in these early days of the Internet era, we were still searching for a name for it. My partner, Todd, used to say in speeches that he would give Polynesian fruit baskets for life to anyone who came up with a single name for the combination of software, knowledge, and work that we were selling. We had moved back east and were scouting out a new headquarters in a historic brick armory building along the Charles River near Boston. Our future looked fabulous, except for one problem: My cousin, the forty-third president of the United States, was about to sign a bill that could destroy us.

This bill, like so many government initiatives, stemmed from the best of intentions. The idea was to encourage the migration of the health care industry from cumbersome binders full of paper to electronic records. How was this to be accomplished? Well, hospitals and doctors were forbidden by a so-called antikickback law from exchanging services, information, or products of value with each other. (It's a law that infuriates me, for reasons I'll go into later.) The bill before Congress in 2004 offered a regulatory safe harbor for hospitals to provide doctors with all the digital technology the bureaucrats could think of: servers, software licenses, and training. That was absolutely the right answer . . . for 1982. Hospitals could buy all the old stuff from our competitors but none of the new, still-to-be-named services from us. As often happens, the technology was advancing much faster than the law.

I caught the Shuttle down to Washington and commenced lobbying with the fervor of a man with a gun to his head. I raced up and down the marble halls of Congress looking for someone, anyone, who would take the time to learn why this bill was so very wrong, so backward, so devastating, so lethal—at least to athenahealth.

But let me tell you, if you walk into congressional offices sputtering about a clause in a bill that practically no one has read, something that has to do with hardware and software and online services, people tend to hurry away, or point you toward the door. I could find no one to pay attention. And as I grew more frantic, I started talking louder and faster. That didn't help things.

Some might find my frustration strange, considering that during this drama my cousin was sitting a mile away, in the Oval Office.

Wouldn't a Bush, facing legislative trouble in Washington, contact someone in the White House entourage? The answer is no. Placing a call to him was not even a remote possibility. For starters, it would have been unethical, and also politically foolish. It would have placed him, me, and my company in scandal and brought shame upon our family. I would have been much more willing to climb the steeple of the tallest church and bungee jump naked in the middle of the night than to call my cousin. And even if I had been dumb enough to make the call, I trust George would have had the good sense to tell me to get lost.

At the time of this drama, my fast-growing company employed hundreds of people in Massachusetts. But I could not get anyone on the state delegation to hear my plea. (It's conceivable that my family name was working against me.) Finally, I located a congresswoman who would listen to me. It was Nancy Johnson, a Republican who had been representing her Connecticut district since 1983. She chaired the health subcommittee of the powerful House Committee on Ways and Means.

I walked into her office and saw the sixty-nine-year-old congresswoman sitting behind a desk. She was paging through an enormous sheaf of papers. That was the bill. Embedded in that piece of legislation were hundreds, if not thousands, of amendments, carmarks, and wrinkles added by one interested party or another, along with thousands of other details that landed there just by dumb luck. Other items, like the all-important clause "and Internet services," were simply missing. It struck me as I watched her paging through this bill that my drama was only one of thousands, or even millions, that would result from this mountain of legislation. A single detail can throw lives or entire companies into a tailspin. It can reroute billions of dollars, turning winners into losers, and vice versa. Government is like a giant with an uzi. It means so well, but if it gets scared or sad or confused, it can squeeze off eighty rounds without even noticing the bodies falling around it. One single law can put technologies that should have disappeared a genera-tion ago onto eternal life support and close the door on their superior replacements. Now, in the last day or two before the bill became law, Representative Johnson was committed to limiting the damage. She was gamely attempting to filter out dangerous bits and pieces. It was exhausting work.

She asked me what I needed. I started my spiel. I went on about hardware and software, and the future of Internet-based businesses, and the importance of medical data traveling across networks. It was the key to efficiency, fairness, the economics of health care, research . . .

"*Stop*," she said. "That's too much for me. What words on what page?"

I pointed to the clause where it said "computers and software," and asked her to add "and Internet services." She did.

Danger averted. Our company would survive this bill.

But let's consider this process for a moment. It has nothing to do with innovation or satisfying customers or delivering great results. It has everything to do with cultivating influence among politicians and regulators. To create a modern, caring, and efficient health care econ-omy, we have to create more spaces where entrepreneurs can compete in the marketplace—and not in the corridors of Capitol Hill.

Unlike many entrepreneurs, I had reason to feel comfortable in Washington. Even though I couldn't call my presidential cousin for help, I had my political name, fancy venture firms behind me, and my equally fancy business degree from Harvard. That gave me the confidence—or hubris—to assume I could get in there and make a difference. I was an outsider with insider status. I'd guess that 90 per-cent of businesses that get blown up by government missteps, or even prevented from being born, are run by outsiders with outsider status. That is why it's so hard for an activist government to be effective. It works with known players—while the future should be in the hands of *unknown* players working to make the household names obsolete.

The government, by regulating industry, actually ends up protecting the incumbents. Here's how. Let's say the news comes out that insurance companies are taking advantage of customers in an especially awful way. Because this is a service that society views as vital, the government comes in and says, "Whoa, what's going on in here?" Now the best thing to do at this point would be to make it as easy as possible for new entrants to come into the system and disrupt these guys—clean their clock, kill them, or at the very least force them to change. But instead the government looks to control them. They do this by writing up cumbersome regulations. These end up discouraging newcomers from the market. Many of the best would-be competitors don't employ a single lobbyist or lawyer. They take one look at a market regulated up the wazoo and conclude, wisely, that they're not built to play that game. They're better off building a new video game or a dating app. So instead of making the bad incumbents vulnerable, the government leaves them fat, lame, and stupid—but with formidable lobbying power. Since these companies employ a lot of people, they become untouchable.

This brings me to my favorite paradox. The industries we care about least innovate at the highest speeds, while those we hold dearest to our heart innovate hardly at all. Education, for example, is perhaps our most precious industry. It prepares our future. And yet it's locked in an archaic system that the signers of the Declaration of Independence would recognize in an instant. Its standard form of delivery, the lecture—literally, the reading—dates from the Middle Ages, when only the teacher had access to a book. Even most new courses online stick to this ancient method.

Health care, the body to education's mind, innovates at the same glacial pace. Meanwhile, industries with no legacy to safeguard—social networks, video games—leap forward week by week.

Now I don't intend to spend this chapter pounding on the government, or proposing a rapid shift to a private health care economy. The government funds and thereby controls half of the industry, through Medicare, Medicaid, and other programs, and it regulates the other half. This is nearly 20 percent of the economy, and people's lives depend on it. It cannot be turned upside down. Radical reforms, from right or left, are bound to be disruptive and sow chaos. What's more, regulations are necessary, though smarter ones than we have today are needed, and only a fraction of the number. The challenge is to regulate in a way that fosters market disruption in the medium term.

For now, I'm not focused on envisioning the perfect system, but instead working with what we have. The key, at least in these early days, is to pry open small doors and windows for entrepreneurs, and to change a few of the most noxious rules and regulations that get in their way. My bet is that once entrepreneurial businesses zero in on customers and quality gets rolling, the public will choose them. Other entrepreneurs and technologists will follow the endless opportunities in health care. Their businesses will sprout, a few will thrive, and the rest of the hulking industry will bend in their direction.

The government can take steps to speed up the transition—and save taxpayers billions in the process. One key is to give consumers more choices, and a bigger financial stake, in managing their health. To understand the dynamics at play, consider a wondrous piece of technology: the proton accelerator. This is the Rolls-Royce of radiation. The machinery occupies a very big room. Its technology sends a beam of ionized protons into cancerous tumors. Like other radiation therapies, this beam lays waste to the DNA of cancer cells, limiting their

ability to reproduce. The benefit of the proton beam is its finely cali-
brated focus. It zaps its target and causes less damage to surrounding
tissue. For this reason, it is the optimal radiation treatment for certain
brain tumors and eye cancers, especially in children. It's also useful for
tumors close to the spinal cord. As you might imagine, it's very expensive. Medicare reimburses about $32,000 for this therapy.

Despite the superior focus of the proton beam, studies indicate that
outside of its specialty—young heads and spinal columns—it doesn't
perform any better than the alternative, IMRT (intensity modulated
radiation therapy). But the proton beam has one huge advantage: It
costs almost twice as much. This may sound counterintuitive. But
imagine that you're at one of the ten hospitals that have invested in this
prodigious tool. It's just sitting there, huge and idle, a $100 million mir-
acle machine waiting for an infant with a certain type of tumor. Days
pass, maybe entire weeks. It's not saving lives. It's not bringing in revenue. It's not coming close to earning its keep.

While the accelerator bides its time, awaiting infants, lots of middle-
aged and elderly men check into the hospitals and clinics in the area
every day. They've been diagnosed with prostate cancer. About a quarter of a million American men get this unwelcome news every year.

You can guess where this story's going. Put yourself in the shoes of
one of these prostate patients. You've been told you have cancer cells in
a part of your body that evokes extremely strong feelings and fears.
You've heard all too much about side effects of cancer therapies, about
incontinence and impotence. You've seen the ads for Depends. Now a
doctor talks to you about your options. We have IMRT, he says. It's the
standard treatment. But luckily, you're just a short drive from the Rolls-
Royce of radiation therapy, a machine with the precision to zap a tumor in a baby's brain. He has one question for you: Which will it be?

Some curious patients might ask the doctor if the proton beam delivers superior results to IMRT. Do fewer of the patients suffer the dreaded side effects? And the doctor, if he's honest, will answer that the differences for prostate cancer, according to recent studies, are negligible. That said, given a choice between a therapy with pinpoint aim and one that's a tad more diffused, why not go for precision? Who knows? Studies coming out in a year or two might prove the superiority of the proton beam. No one suggests that it's worse.

And this brings you to the central question: Will it cost *me* any more?

To which the doctor smiles, gives a reassuring pat on the shoulder, and says, "No. Medicare picks it up."

Case closed. We're going with the Rolls-Royce.

Versions of this minidrama have been played out thousands of times over recent years. Prostate cancer is manna for hospitals that bought proton accelerators; the hefty insurance reimbursements help to amortize the investments. In some hospitals, prostates account for 70 percent of the massive machine's labor. Our taxes and insurance premiums underwrite this extremely expensive therapy, which costs nearly twice as much as another that is equally effective.

In a true market, this would not happen. The price would dive below the cost of financing and operating the fancy machine, until inefficient players were forced from the market. At the same time, the consumer would have a financial stake in the dealings, and access to relevant information. None of us would pay twice as much for a flat-screen TV or a washing machine unless we had information indicating that it worked a whole lot better. If two items or services are about the same, going with the cheaper one is a no-brainer—unless someone else is paying for it. That's what happens in health care. Those of us with insurance don't have skin in the game. If we did, if we were spending our own money, our choices would force the market into competing on price and quality and customer service. That's what shoppers demand.

In the case of many cancers, even I have to concede that a pure shopping model won't work, at least not yet. Cancer therapies cost too much for all but the very rich. This isn't like other consumer decisions, like reroofing the house, buying a car, or even replacing a knee. It's more like losing a house to a hurricane. Insurance has to pay.

Yet even in the most costly treatments, we could introduce market forces—if the government would let us. The key is to give the customer a chance to share in the savings.

Let's return to that discussion between the doctor and the prostate patient. Imagine that after delivering the good news that Medicare will pick up the bill for the proton beam, the doctor informs the patient about an enticement: If the patient opts for the cheaper treatment, he'll get to split the savings with the insurer. That's $7,000, right into his pocket.

If this sounds too good to be true, it is. This type of enticement is illegal under current law. Why? Quite simply, government officials do not trust patients to inform themselves and make smart decisions. The introduction of market incentives could introduce extraneous items like monstrous credit-card balances into a decision that should be about nothing but the patient's health. And yet, it could be argued that the hospital's nudge to use the proton accelerator for prostate cancer has much more to do with amortizing a questionable investment than the patient's tumor.

Looking at it cynically, it boils down to this: Why should the patient get to dip into the trough when the hospital needs the money so badly? And while we're at it, why trust the patients to make smart decisions in the first place? Look at them. They smoke like chimneys, drink like fish, and eat like pigs. They're couch potatoes. They blow out their credit cards and buy houses they can't afford. If we start offering them rebates for choosing cheaper treatments, some will no doubt forgo treatment for stage-four liver cancer and use the rebate to bankroll a monthlong bacchanalia in Las Vegas.

Then again, if that is how a person chooses to close out his or her time on earth, who are we to say no?

In a world in which all of us die, what exactly are the risks we should be measuring and minimizing with our laws and regulations? Is it premature death? Pain? Inconvenience? I think each one of us has a different answer and would thrive in a system that offers loads of options, along with plentiful data to make informed choices. This in turn would give birth to a market that would provide even more choices, including many we haven't even dreamed of. Yet laws, even well-intentioned ones like the three thousand pages in the Obamacare bill, tend to reduce choices and bolster the bloated incumbents, from hospitals to pharmaceutical giants, that created this mess in the first place.

What about the people's "right" to health care? I agree with a very limited version of that premise. I would say that everyone should be covered for the kinds of treatments and therapies that the vast majority of Americans cannot afford. That would include serious accidents and curable catastrophic illnesses. But the rest of the smorgasbord? I'd let people choose. They conceivably could reduce premiums dramatically by buying only the insurance they want. Smorgasbords, on the other hand, make people insensitive to price and tolerant of indifferent service. In short, it discourages shopping.

I'm reminded of this every time I go to a hotel offering "free" breakfast. Usually, it's an all-you-can-eat buffet. Once I've paid the $300 plus four different taxes for the room, am I going to venture out and shop for breakfast, or stay put and eat for free? Most people stick with the buffet, figuring correctly that they've paid for it. In some towns, I'd imagine, the dominance of the hotel buffet discourages local entrepreneurs from starting up their own breakfast cafés. How could they ever compete for a captive customer base? And with scant local competition, the hotel faces little pressure to improve on the hard and tasteless chunks of cantaloupe and honeydew melon in their fruit salad or to upgrade the "maple flavored" corn syrup people swab on their waffles. The quality is often wretched. But I've noticed that some customers compensate by overconsuming. Some start with fruit and muffins, go back for eggs and bacon, and crown the experience with pancakes warmed under a heat lamp for an hour. With an eye to lunch, some even pocket a few bagels and an apple or two. Hey, it's free.

Much the same happens with all-you-can-eat health care. People have severely limited choices, and the service is often mediocre, or worse. But they consume a lot of health care. After all, it's already been paid for, along with a lot of stuff they don't want or need.

As a consequence, about one quarter of the average American's life income, by some estimates, is taken away and placed into health care. I cannot believe for a moment that millions of Americans would choose that allocation. They'd likely say, "What do I get for 20 percent? What do I get for 15 percent?" In this case, different grab bags of coverage would emerge to suit the varying budgets and values of the country.

I'd also point out that many people who benefit from more choices will make the most of them. And I'm not talking only about folks stocking up on kale and carrots at Whole Foods. Given more freedom and responsibility, all kinds of people will shop for the services they need. They'll inform themselves by means of the exploding marketplace of information and data about health care. Many of them will end up spending less on health—and with far better results—than they get today. They'll share their successes and disappointments in e-mails and on social networks. The market will grow more sophisticated. And people's choices will define their values and priorities, their humanity.

But first they have to clear a host of obstacles, many of them erected by governments. Let's imagine one of these new health care shoppers has a problem with her eye. Something's blurry. She lives near me, in

Massachusetts, and goes to one of the many great doctors we have. He tells her to get an MRI. She has a super high deductible, which means the price is going to be coming out of her pocket. So she shops. She finds that some places charge three times as much as others. But still, even the cheap ones cost a lot, about $600 for a single MRI. She does more research and learns that the state government actually forbids new companies from setting up shop and offering competing services. Why would this be? The justification is that they don't want society to overinvest in certain technologies. We shouldn't build more than we need.

Think how different that is from restaurants. There might be six eateries on a single block, and a seventh opens up because that entrepreneur has the hope, the belief (and often the delusion), that he or she will create something better, that this seventh restaurant will outperform the other six. This is wonderful for consumers. Sure, it has its destructive side. More than half of restaurant start-ups go belly-up in year one, and according to a study by the Perry Group, 70 percent of those that make it past the first year are shut down within five years. The free market claims plenty of victims while creating value for consumers. State laws that shield imaging centers and hospitals from competition deprive the public of the one force—competition—that would drive down prices and improve service. We need a lot more death in the provider space.

And don't get me started on state lines. They undermine the promise of a national health care market. They run across the economy like so many fences, dividing the market into fiefdoms, which almost always hurt the consumer. Let's say you live in New Jersey and find a better insurance plan across the river in New York. Sorry. You're out of luck. But don't worry, you're told. Your state insurance regulators are doing their job, upholding standards and protecting your interests. Naturally, they can't protect you in another state. So you pay more.

This makes little sense. You regularly cross the Hudson River for dinner on the town—and entrust your health to New York restaurant regulators. You drive through a tunnel and count on highway safety as regulated by New York's Department of Motor Vehicles. But out-of-staters cannot buy insurance there. Ask yourself this: Who are those laws protecting?

These geographic limitations also subvert the promise of the information economy. Let's say someone in Wyoming develops a pink lump under the skin on his forearm. He doesn't know that it's an aggressive skin cancer called Merkel cell carcinoma, which strikes only 1,200 Americans per year. Chances are, the local radiologist in Cheyenne, Cody, or Detroit, for that matter, has never seen such a lump. But with a cloud-based service, the patient can send this image to a specialist, perhaps in Florida or the backwoods of Maine. This expert focuses exclusively on subcutaneous lumps. She sees hundreds of them every day, from all over the country. She gets constant practice and develops world-class expertise. She identifies the carcinoma. In this example, the network provides scale to build human expertise, which serves up the answer, just as it should.

But wait! Before this expert looks at the image, one question: Does she have a license to practice in Wyoming? Believe it or not, in cloud-based diagnostic centers today, each image must be entrusted only to experts licensed in the state where the patient lives. This adds cost and slows down the growth of services that would benefit all of us. Couldn't states agree to cross-certify? Sure they could. But it might undermine their local businesses. So once again, inefficiency is protected, a local job or two is saved, and the public is denied the best possible service.

Underlying much of this legislation is a fear that some devious companies will be benefiting from their relationships with patients. Profiteers will emerge. Of course, this is absurd, given that all sorts of companies, from pharmaceutical giants to "nonprofit" hospitals, earn a good living in protected fiefdoms (and channel a portion of this lucre into campaign contributions). Still, despite all of the wealth sloshing around in health care, there's a resistance to market activities that are commonplace—and essential—in other industries.

The one issue that sends me into fits has to do with data. As you know, information has value. Every time you use a credit card or withdraw money from an ATM, information about you zips across a network of banks, retailers, credit bureaus. The seller has to know that you're good for the money, and it is ready to pay, usually just a few pennies, for this information. Without it, global commerce would grind to a halt.

Yet in health care, we have what are known as antikickback laws. The idea is to outlaw side deals, where businesses in cahoots send each other contracts or patients. These laws certainly have a valid goal.

Yet they prevent health care from developing a robust and efficient information network. Let's say you move from Houston to Chicago and go to a new doctor. She wants to know what medication you've been on for the last five years, and you can't find the piece of paper where you have all the medications written down. In a modern system, one designed to the highest privacy standards, she would be able to retrieve in a second or two the digital record from your doctor's office in Texas and pay perhaps a few bucks for the service.

This type of payment lays the foundation for an information industry. Where does it lead? Maybe a technology company buys access to millions of patient records and develops a system to deliver the information, with security and speed, at a fraction of the cost, a nickel or even a penny. This would provide immense benefits for all of us. Quickly, new business models would emerge in a vibrant medical data economy. But it won't happen as long as payment for information remains illegal.

Now many of the people who sat down in 2009 to draft the behemoth that became known as Obamacare wanted to strip these inefficiencies from the health care economy. They understood that the promise of universal care hinged upon making the system work better and cheaper, and many of them believed that introducing transparency and competition was key. They wanted to reduce geographic and political fiefdoms. They understood that antikickback laws needed to be pruned. I know some of these people. We talked. They tried very hard. Yet each one of their market-based reforms was weakened, neutered, or jettisoned during the legislative process.

An example. The Obama team had its eyes on one of the horrors of the health care economy: unbridled fee for service. This is the scheme in which the medical practice charges patients for every billable event— every bandage, every drug, every liter of saline solution, every bedside chat. Fee for service creates invoices that go on for ten or fifteen pages, and prices that are off the charts. What's worse, they focus the attention of medical professionals more on creating billable events than tending to the needs of the patient. Fee for service embodies the worst in American health care.

It doesn't have to be. In fact, fee for service would be OK if patients could get a sense of what they were buying and opt out if they chose to, or demand other options. In the rest of the economy, that is known as product management. We seem to have it everywhere but in health care.

The Obama team wanted to create an alternative to fee for service. So they pushed a new scheme called Accountable Care Organization, or ACO. Very similar to an existing program, Medicare Advantage, ACO groups get paid with the normal fee for service. However, the total spend for all their patients is tallied during the course of the year. If the total fee-for-service spending goes down by enough, the ACO gets half of the savings as a bonus.

This sounds promising. But then come the conditions. For example, it turns out that each ACO has to be 75 percent owned by the providers participating in it, which means mostly doctors. This amendment, of course, came from the doctors' lobby, and it promptly weakened the ACO as a competitive player. Why? Think back to our business model for birthing at Athena Women's Health. One of the keys to cutting costs was to minimize the participation of doctors, and to employ them only when the situation called for the highest level of expertise. Midwives were better suited for most of the work, and cost one third as much. Some of the doctor-owned ACOs will no doubt see the logic of hiring midwives and medics. Others won't. But by limiting opportunities to doctor-owned groups, the law prevents legions of outsiders from crashing the party and providing much-needed disruption.

Worse, by restricting ACO ownership to practitioners, the law effectively bars outsiders from the industry. And outsiders are precisely what health care needs. Health care is starving for efficiency experts, customer service geniuses, retail mavens, people who have created thriving and modern businesses in other industries, and will apply their expertise to health care. In a brilliant *New Yorker* article, "Big Med," published on August 13, 2012, Atul Gawande explores efficiency and quality control at The Cheesecake Factory restaurants. They have it down to a science. This is the work of brainy product managers, the same kind who figure out how to sell us two-year phone subscriptions and supersized burgers. They're the outsiders who should be landing at ACOs. But the law keeps them out. As usual, when it comes to legislation, the incumbents come out on top.

You might think that there would be one exception, one government initiative I'd be crazy not to love. That would be the original 2009 Health Information Technology for Economic and Clinical Health (or HITECH) Act—part of the economic stimulus package, which committed $39 billion to underwrite the switch to electronic health records (EHRs). This spurred a surge in tech investments, by hospitals and medical groups, and it no doubt benefited athenahealth, as well as our competitors.

But you know what? If the industry were open to real market competition, companies would have to make those investments just to survive. Have you ever noticed, for example, that every McDonald's and Burger King runs on computers? Those companies didn't need any incentives. The idea of providing great service without this technology is unthinkable. A restaurant chain that relied on shouted orders, handwritten notes, and file cabinets would be dead within a month.

In health care, by contrast, many practices had no compelling reason to switch to digital systems. Many doctors grumbled about them. More important, they weren't facing agile Internet-based competitors. So why change? Sure, patients complained when they were given a clipboard and a pen and asked to fill in the same information for the tenth or twentieth time. But the resistance from doctors counted more than the gripes from patients. Plus, there were vague privacy concerns about electronic health records. So the status quo stuck.

Now if medical businesses received a clear sign from the marketplace that going digital was the key to survival, they presumably would take the decision with great rigor. A faulty system, after all, could sink them. They would study the alternatives, figure out which option fit their business model. They would work to turn a glaring vulnerability into a comparative advantage. They'd have to, or they'd die.

But that wasn't the message. With the HITECH Act, the government was literally paying them to go digital. So most of them complied.

Some subscribed to services like ours. Others went into buying mode. They ran to the companies they knew, the ones that had sales forces and golf outings, and they bought a lot of technology that predated the Internet. For many, it didn't make much difference, because it didn't come with a commitment to change their business operations. Some of what they bought provides some value. But a lot of it is technology they never really wanted, which they'll eventually throw out.

While I was working on this chapter, I had a chance to talk with Bob Kocher. He's a doctor and is now a partner at the venture firm Venrock, working on health care tech investments. In 2009, he worked for the Obama administration and wrote most of the original Affordable Care Act. You might be surprised to learn that Bob and I agree broadly about the market reforms needed for health care (though he sees a larger role for government than I do). In any case, I wanted to hear it from Bob: What went wrong? Here are some excerpts of our conversation.

Bush: Why does the ACO have to be 75 percent owned by doctors? You're allowed to build a new entity to disrupt the market, but you have to be 75 percent owned—

Kocher: And report sixty-five quality measures, and get paid eighteen months later. The Medicare shared savings program is totally unattractive. I worked on that. It bums me out.

Bush: But what happened? Tell us how you went—

Kocher: There's this amazing concern that doctors will unethically ration care, and act against their patients' interests, by telling them, "Don't go to Dana Farber for your cancer, because it costs too much money." That led Medicare to push for extra controls. So there has to be a patient representative from the community and a bunch of extra governance to make sure the ACO is acting in a patient-beneficial way. There's this doubt that the market would punish practices by not sending patients to them. It seems to me that the way to do this—and I pushed for it and didn't succeed—was to make the performance really transparent. People won't want to go to the bad doctors. But Medicare, in this paternalistic way, felt that patients don't understand the data, and that the data won't be perfect in integrity enough to allow people to see that.

Bush: One thing that drives me crazy is a regulation or a code that locks in an obsolete procedure or technology.

Kocher: Dialysis is a really good example, because we have a substitute treatment that actually works better: home dialysis and abdominal peritoneal dialysis. But instead, we hook you up to machines that take all of your blood out.

Bush: We drive to the center. We pick you up in an ambulance—

Kocher: Yes, we drive you to a facility, of which there are far too many, and hook you up to a machine for three hours. You have to sit there and watch Oprah, or whatever they have on. Now instead of that, you could do home dialysis, by yourself, with no caregivers, like the rest of the world does, for basically the cost of saline solution. But we have this whole infrastructure around dialysis because we have payments that go to it. Now we have buildings with all these nurses—

Bush: Those are jobs! So if you [switch to the new procedure], you're basically going to a publicly traded company with thousands of employees and saying, "We're shutting you down." It's like a military base closing, a government decision that wipes out jobs. But this one would change the game for a profitable and successful community of companies.

Kocher: It can't be done.

Bush: Did this dialysis issue come up while working on the health care bill?

Kocher: No. This is such a good idea that we couldn't talk about it. And if you look at the lobbying power of big companies like Amgen, you can see what we were facing. They have the largest, smartest, and best-connected lobbyists of any company I know. And I think, at one point, they had given more money than any other company to the Senate Finance Committee. Now Amgen sells this drug called Epogen. It's a drug that makes your blood grow. Dialysis actually degrades your blood. So the government pays the dialysis centers to administer this drug. And the drug is even more profitable than the dialysis. They charge thousands of dollars for it. You could just eat spinach, or iron, and probably get most of the benefit. But for years, Amgen has been able to lobby for really high Medicare payments for it. And in budget negotiations when we were facing the fiscal cliff [in late 2012], [Sen.] Max Baucus [D-Mont.] put in a provision to pull out the cuts to Epogen. And Amgen's lobbyists did magic to get two years of price protection for another dialysis drug, Sensibar. That was a windfall for Amgen, which was worth about $500 million in revenue.

Bush: Here's the problem. These are middle-class, good jobs. And because they're good jobs that run through the individual fingers of the congressman, the congressman cannot let them go. Look at a job in a market economy. If a company goes under, and the government is just in the role of regulator, the congressman can say, "It's not my fault that your stuff costs twice as much and isn't any better." It would never occur to anyone that that would be any congressman's fault. But all of a sudden, because the dollar is pulled by force away from the buyer and run through this one choke point, now the congressman's fingerprint is on everything that's at risk. It's structurally and physically impossible for a Republican or a Democrat to take it away.

Kocher: I think we need something outside government to tell Medicare that they have to stop paying for dialysis, and for the proton beam. Because Congress will never do it. And Medicare can't, because if Medicare tried, Congress would have an oversight hearing where they'd beat the crap out of Medicare, and it would get put back. So we need an outside body, a payment advisory board.

Bush: That's magical thinking. The idea that somebody can be outside of government, but still be advising the government on what to do with its centralized power. It can't happen. . . .

By the way, is it illegal to cut a check to a patient for choosing the cheaper thing? If I'm fully at risk, as a doctor. I've got global cap. Can I say, "Listen, I want you to go to this colonoscopy and not that one. I'll give you fifty bucks if you go there."

Kocher: In Medicare, it's illegal to do that. You can't give a patient an inducement, a reward, an incentive, and that's—

Bush: Tragic.

Kocher: It's bullshit. The worry is that, just like homeless people sell their sperm and their plasma, poor people will go to the horrible place. But doctors don't want to send you to a horrible place. It's not in my interest, as a doctor, to send you to the bad place. Even economically it doesn't make sense. Unless you die right away, the bad place will cost more, because there's a bigger chance you'll be hospitalized. But government says, "We won't let you pay the patient to go to the right place, even give him the taxi ride, because it might create a situation in which you'll do the wrong thing for the money."

Bush: So how do you look at your work on this law? That you had one crack at the apple and were trying to get some market going?

Kocher: Yeah, and it makes me sad. The way I rationalize my work is that we knew what made sense. [Obama's chief economic adviser] Larry Summers and I would sit down, and we knew what the right answer was. We knew what the current answer was. We were 99 percent away from where we thought we should be, and we narrowed it to 80 percent. That was the politically possible. Then we lost some ground, because the implementation was uneven and crappy. So we're down to 15 percent of what we wanted to do.

PART
TWO

Disrupting the Ecosystem

CHAPTER FIVE

Tottering Titans

Not long ago, I was talking to the directors of a large pediatric hospital. It's one of the best in the world. A host of world-class surgeons there carry out the most delicate and sophisticated operations on children and babies, sometimes even fetuses. It's a miracle factory, and it's brimming with all the technology you could hope for. As you can imagine, this is an expensive enterprise to keep afloat, and like most hospitals, it's looking for new avenues of growth, new revenue streams. When I was there, the board was discussing the possibility of buying pediatric practices throughout their region. That would expand their footprint, and bring more patients through their doors.

"Don't do that!" I told them. "It's an outrageous waste." What you have to do, I said, is focus on what you're the best at, and build a market around that. By simply expanding their regional footprint, they would be growing their commodity business—the stuff most hospitals are terrible at.

Their faces fell. Here they were looking to grow, and it sounded as though I was telling them to shrink.

I explained. There's a condition called atrial septic defect (ASD). This is when a baby is born with a hole in the wall between the two upper chambers of the heart. Usually, the hole closes itself over time. But in serious cases, the baby requires surgery. Very few hospitals in the country have the expertise and equipment in place to perform this surgery as well as this hospital I was visiting. It's a specialty there, and the procedure costs well over $100,000. The trouble, from a business perspective, is that serious cases of atrial septic defect are relatively rare. If this hospital tried to expand its local ASD market, the star surgeons would have little to do most days but check for new golf apps on their iPads.

So I gave them my suggestion for building a market: Buy a jet and offer ASD at $80,000—a 20 percent discount. Turn yourselves into the ASD destination for every child within a thousand miles. Fly whole families in. Put them up at the Marriott for a week. It might cost $10,000, but you'll earn it back. You'll grab the ASD market share and, in the process, get valuable practice. As you work at it, you'll not only get better at the surgery but will also figure out how to streamline the process. I'm betting the hospital could cut the cost of ASD surgery by $20,000, even $30,000—and that drops straight to the bottom line.

Maybe, I said, the ASD practice would grow to occupy a floor of the hospital, maybe more. So how to free up the space for it? Jettison all the businesses that everyone else can do just as well, all the tests and procedures that should be done by medics in neighborhood clinics, or at Walgreens or Target. There's no need for world-class surgeons to waste their time on commodity treatment—for which hospitals charge twice or three times as much.

I don't know if this pediatric hospital will eventually take my advice. My bet, though, is that rising competition will force major hospitals to radically shift their business model—or to die. Some of them will go belly-up, and—though it may sound cruel—that will be a good thing for our health and our economy.

Even while doctors and nurses and other professionals have been doing loads of fabulous work, saving lives and performing the occasional miracle, their institutions have also been bleeding us dry, especially over the last two decades. Their status quo—the hospital as a do-it-all department store—is unsustainable. Outside of their specialties, most of them simply are not great at what they do. They're inefficient, wasteful, and they often deliver frightful customer service. They overcharge. In fact, it's part of the business model. I do not blame them for this. They are trying to carry on the important work they do, and for this they adjust to the distortions of our health care economy. For example, hospitals reward and reimburse procedures, but not cures. In fact, health care should be largely about promoting and sustaining health, a job for which most hospitals are singularly ill-equipped.

Hospital executives understand all too well that when customers can shop and compare prices and service, their business model, already troubled, will suffer. So many of them are busy trying to lock up market share, developing monopolies and duopolies, and overcharging. This has to stop, and it will.

This drama has been playing virtually nonstop in the Boston area for the last twenty years. I live in Cambridge, Massachusetts, about a twelve-minute walk from Harvard Yard. If I get on my bike, I can ride in fifteen minutes to six—count 'em—big research hospitals. We have Beth Israel, Brigham and Women's, Children's, Boston Medical, Tufts, and the big kahuna, Massachusetts General. These tertiary centers provide a full complement of services, from obstetrics to transplants. When a patient is in big trouble in a regional hospital, he or she might get helicoptered to a tertiary. They're usually connected to a university and are renowned for research. Most of them are nonprofits—though that is largely a distinction for accounting purposes.

Each tertiary center, much like a cathedral, sits atop an ecosystem. Surrounding it is a host of lowlier institutions, some in suburbs or old mill towns, others in grittier neighborhoods. While a typical tertiary center has marble flooring in its lobby and various wings and pavilions named after donors, a community hospital might have linoleum flooring and a more modest wing named after a congressman who threw a bone its way, or maybe a revered priest. If the tertiary hospital is the central pole of the ecosystem, the community hospitals are often satellites. Beyond them are a host of clinics and specialty practices. All of them feed into, and sustain, the name-brand hospital.

In this section of four chapters, we're going to explore this ecosystem. Over the last decades, it has ossified into a hierarchy, one in which everyone knows his or her place. But that order, with the research hospital presiding at the very top, is under siege. Even in an industry as estranged from market forces as health care, people still want to make a buck. And that's fueling a Darwinian process in which lots of players are after someone else's lunch. We'll look in this chapter at a chain of community hospitals laying siege to research giants in Boston. Then we'll see how a couple of entrepreneurial obstetricians in Florida have used savvy strategy, information technology, and a focus on customer service to build a regional giant of childbirth. Who do they take business away from? Hospitals. On another ring are national retailers, like Target, CVS, and Walgreens, running clinics for coughs, scrapes, checkups, and tests. They're after a piece of the same $2.7 trillion market and—again—they wrest business from every incumbent player, from hospitals to regional clinics and medical practices.

The ecosystem also features revolutionaries and innovators. We'll look at one innovator who is zeroing in on the chronically ill, a market that accounts for a dizzying 75 percent of health care spending, according to the Centers for Disease Control. His approach is to shower patients with primary care—and keep them out of hospitals. Another innovator, this one in New York's Adirondack Mountains, is helping customers manage their conditions so effectively that the local hospital's business is declining. Even in this remote nook of the health care ecosystem, the hospital's business is vulnerable. This Darwinian drama will force hospitals to adapt or disappear. Many will succumb.

These battles are already under way, and most of us are already participating. Consider one hypothetical scenario involving shopping. Let's say you need a CT scan. On the one hand, there's a new imaging center in a strip mall not far from your house, in the carcass of an old Blockbuster. They charge $150, and your insurance covers it. Now if you prefer the traditional alternative, you can drive downtown to the big prestigious medical center, pay $20 for parking, and get your CT scan done there. It costs $500, and your copay must cover a big chunk of the difference. It's exactly the same equipment, but it comes with the brand of a world-class hospital. Which option do you choose?

This is a hospital's worst nightmare. If someone shops around—whether it's customers themselves, general practitioners, or insurers directing groups of patients—the resulting competition will erode the hospital's fat profit belly, eviscerating its business model. It is starting to happen.

I'll begin at the top of this food chain, starting in my hometown. Twenty years ago in Boston, while I was still consulting at Booz Allen, Massachusetts General had a problem. Health maintenance organizations were flexing their power in the market and pushing for lower rates. This was during that brief period in the nineties when health care spending actually declined. HMOs were telling Mass General that if they didn't lower rates, they'd simply send patients to a competing tertiary center. From Mass General's perspective, there was too much competition in the regional market.

The big kahuna reduced this competition with a historic merger. It teamed up with Brigham and Women's, creating a single enterprise,

Partners HealthCare. Even in a hospital haven like Boston, this was a powerful combination. Insurers felt enormous pressure to include Partners in their coverage. Following the merger, Partners won big rate hikes from Blue Cross Blue Shield of Massachusetts. Emboldened, in 2000 it demanded a 30 percent increase over three years from Tufts Health Plan, claiming that Tufts's business had accounted for $42 million in losses over the two previous years. Tufts balked. It saw that only 12 percent of its customers made use of Partners. And since the area was teeming with tertiary centers, customers could go elsewhere for their care, right?

Wrong. With Partners no longer in its network, Tufts found itself in a tough spot. Maybe only a fraction of its customers made use of Partners, but many more of them demanded the right to. If these customers came down with leukemia or lupus, they wanted access to the world-famous hospitals, the miracle factories. Who wouldn't when the stakes are life and death?

Tufts soon saw that the appeal of Partners, and its power, extended far beyond the 12 percent who actually went there. And these people made lots of noise. What's worse, Tufts's timing was disastrous. The showdown with Partners occurred just as the Tufts health plan was entering its largest open enrollment period of the year. Customers might bail. Before long, Tufts relented and agreed to the steep rate hikes.

"That was a big turning point," says my friend Charlie Baker, who at the time was CEO of Harvard Pilgrim Health Care. "We all saw that if people can't go to Partners, they complain to HR."

Over the following decade, Partners continued to thrive. They often were able to charge premium rates for ordinary tests and procedures like colonoscopies and CT scans. They then followed the standard path of prosperous nonprofits. They built more pavilions. They continued to hire top specialists. They paid themselves richly. And yes, they plunged into more cutting-edge research, which they continued to bankroll in part through premium pricing for commodity services.

Throughout the country, the Partners' model has been spreading. Hospitals are merging like mad, trying desperately to eliminate regional competitors. There were 551 mergers between 2007 and 2012, and the number is rising. While 50 hospital mergers took place in 2009, the figure more than doubled, to 105, by 2012. Giants are getting bigger. New York's Mount Sinai Medical Center gobbled up Beth Israel, St. Luke's, and Roosevelt hospitals. Dallas's Tenet Healthcare, a regional powerhouse, bought Nashville's Vanguard Health Systems, a network of twenty-eight hospitals. Booz Allen, my old employer, predicts that one out of five hospitals will seek out mergers by 2020. I'd say that's a conservative guess.

At the same time, big hospitals are extending their dominance by buying local medical practices by the hundreds. In the first decade of this century, the number of doctors employed by hospitals rose by nearly 75 percent, according to a study by the Medical Group Management Association. And the trend is accelerating. The percentage of cardiologists working for hospitals tripled between 2007 and 2012. Naturally, these doctors funnel streams of their patients into the same hospitals. Each patient brings the potential for a lifetime stream of revenue. A 2013 study by Merritt Hawkins and Associates shows that physicians are generating $4.65 in hospital revenue for each $1 of salary. The average orthopedic surgeon, for example, receives a salary of $485,000 and brings in business worth $2.1 million per year. This is known as "feeding the beast." For many hospitals, this revenue still doesn't cover costs. But it does extend their dominance.

So what gives? Am I accusing these big hospitals of evil? Not at all. They're no worse than the rest of us. But they suffer from an affliction that affects only the most successful players in a mature industry. I call it Upper Right Quadrant Syndrome, or URQS. This occurs when companies fear that they've exhausted the possibility of growing their business by offering new products and services, or appealing to new customers. So they proceed to various forms of coercion. URQS is devastating, both for customers and the greater marketplace. It crushes new players and snuffs out innovation. URQS, as you can imagine, runs rampant in health care.

For a simple view of URQS, imagine a new grocery in a remote town. It's up against a big store that's been there forever. Now picture a chart with an X- and a Y-axis. X represents revenue, Y market share. On day one, the new store has zero of each. It's nestled in the extreme lower-left-hand quadrant. Then it starts to land customers, who come in for discounted milk and eggs. Revenue trickles in. Market share climbs. On the chart, the store moves up and to the right. Still, plenty of potential customers hold off. They stick with the old store. So the start-up innovates. It launches cooking classes on Tuesday nights. It brings in new lines of organic vegetables. Its reputation rises. More customers come in, revenue continues to grow. The line moves up and to the right.

Then there comes a day when the old store closes shop. The upstart has won. Now look at its chart. Revenue is high and market share is dominant. There's no other store within thirty miles. The grocery store is firmly ensconced in the upper right. How is it going to grow now? Well, it could spread to other towns, attracting new customers. Or it could innovate, coming up with new services and products to offer its existing customer base. But both those options are risky. They hinge on winning in a competitive marketplace. The other choice is simpler: to raise prices on existing products.

This is what URQS is all about. Growth comes from leveraging dominance in the marketplace. You used to see it a lot in the tech industry, where companies sold software that worked only on their own machines. They eliminated choice and attempted to lock in customers. The Internet has broken down many of those barriers. But URQS remains the classic business model in much of the health care industry.

Now if the growing hospitals were like other behemoths in the market economy—Walmart, say, or Amazon—we might be wringing our hands over the pitiless power of markets. The big ones, which are more efficient, gobble up the small fry, or bury them. We lose the human contact of the local store. But in most cases, there is an upside: We usually gain lower prices and a bigger selection—more choice. In the medical example, which is decidedly not a real market, that upside vanishes. As big ones take over the small, prices shoot up. Choices vanish. It's as if water flowed uphill. It's the victory of the inefficient. And hospitals, which touch only 5 percent of the population in any given year, have managed to exert their influence over the other 95 percent.

What's worse, as big research hospitals buy community hospitals or medical practices, they position themselves for higher payments from insurers. Here's why. A tertiary center is permitted to charge more for a basic procedure because it helps to underwrite valuable medical research. This is called a "facility fee." So as many of these hospitals spread, they can also impose facility fees at the community hospitals they acquire. Why not? It supports their research, which they house in new pavilions, some of them designed by celebrity architects. It's win-win, boosters argue. The hospital expands, the city gains prestige, a shiny addition to its skyline, and more high-paying jobs.

Well, consumers are left to foot the bill—with higher premiums, fees, and taxes. Some might choose to support the research hospital. It does great research, has a fabulous reputation for conquering deadly diseases, and is a pillar of the local economy (though it often doesn't pay much in the way of taxes). But in the current setup, it's not a choice at all. Money simply flows toward the hospital. H. Gilbert Welch, a professor at Dartmouth's Institute for Health Policy and Clinical Practice, points to a typical example. Duke University's health system in North Carolina has been buying up cardiology practices in the area. This helped to lift the number of echocardiograms performed in the hospital by 68 percent in a single year. And since Duke is a research hospital, it was able to jack up the Medicare reimbursement for these exams from $200 to $471. This is classic URQS.

Hospitals are doing this less from greed than from desperation. Their markets are shrinking. Even as our population ages, we're spending fewer nights in hospital beds. It's about a 1 percent decline every year. This is due in part to the growth of outpatient treatments. Plus, insurance companies are pushing hospitals to cycle out patients faster, reducing their financial exposure. This will continue. According to a study from Dartmouth, we're still using 45 percent more beds than medical needs would justify.

While many hospitals bring in more revenue by gobbling up medical practices and hiring doctors, it's still not enough. A 2011 study in the *New England Journal of Medicine* argues that hiring a single doctor loses hospitals an average of $150,000 per year for the first three years. To break even, a primary care doctor must generate at least 30 percent more visits than he or she does at the outset. Specialists must pick up another 25 percent of referrals. After three years, they come closer to breaking even, but still operate in the red.

You might wonder why this is. Many of these hospitals have dominant market share. Legions of doctors funnel patients through their doors, for routine exams and to see specialists. They charge them high prices. Yet many of them struggle financially. They'll argue that it's because of the expensive research they do, the new pavilions they build, and the money they lose caring for the uninsured. But that's only part of it. The real reason is that they've never had to operate as a business. They don't know how. They haven't been disrupted.

Consider this: In 1990, according to Bob Kocher, there were ten people supporting each doctor in America. Some, like nurses, helped with patient care. Others, such as administrators, receptionists, and technicians, kept the business running. In the quarter century since then, we've had a computer revolution. We've gone online. Millions of jobs have been automated and outsourced. But in that same quarter century, hospital staffs have become bloated, and now there are sixteen people supporting each doctor. Half of them are administrators. This isn't just negative productivity, it's insanity.

Just picture the inefficiency. A single patient lies in a hospital bed. A doctor walks in with sixteen other people. That patient's bill not only must underwrite all of the fabulous technology in the hospital, and its research, but it must also pay the salaries and benefits of that large contingent that can barely squeeze into the room. In Boston, Kocher says, there are one and a half people writing software full time for each hospital bed.

Now if you look at this scene from the point of view of an entrepreneur, it's dripping with potential. All you have to do is to bite off a chunk of that hospital business, reduce the overhead, and offer good services at reasonable rates. It's still true, of course, that most individuals are still not shopping for cheaper services, but insurance companies will pay attention, won't they? Don't employers want to lower their bills?

This brings us to the next ring of the ecosystem, to the community hospitals. What can they steal away from the Partners of the world?

In Massachusetts, we have a front-row seat to such a drama. In 2010, the private-equity firm Cerberus Capital bought a struggling chain of six Catholic hospitals, Caritas Christi Health Care, from the Boston

Archdiocese. Caritas was the second-largest chain in New England, and was made up of community hospitals with virtually no brand appeal. But Cerberus saw this humble and cash-poor grouping as a vehicle to capture a share of the billions pouring into overpriced health services at big research hospitals. There had to be a way to siphon off some of that business. So Cerberus turned Caritas into a for-profit business and re-named it Steward Health. It has now grown to eleven hospitals.

If you return to our department store analogy, Partners and Steward are both in the same business. Partners is an upscale store downtown, maybe Saks Fifth Avenue. Steward, by contrast, looks to make its money more like Target, offering quality at a lower price closer to home. Steward goes to employers who are struggling to pay rising health care bills and offers them a deal: Steward will take an entire insured workforce and cut its bills by 20 percent or more. The idea, which is especially appealing to companies that self-insure their employees, takes on the risk of the entire population. It accepts a fixed amount per patient, and makes its money by providing more efficient treatments. According to Ralph de la Torre, the CEO of Steward, checking into a tertiary center for a routine ailment is like "taking your Ford to the Ferrari Formula 1 garage for repairs."

At this point, you're probably left with one vital question: If angry customers drove Tufts back into the arms of Partners, how can Steward avoid the same trouble? The short answer is that Steward cannot. De la Torre knew from the start that Steward's business model focused on the 99 percent of the care that a good community hospital can deliver. However, the toughest 1 percent of the cases would require the expertise and technology of a tertiary hospital. For this, de la Torre had to find a tertiary partner. Fortunately, with his 1.2 million annual customers, he had more leverage than Tufts did. So he held a bake-off. He asked all the tertiary centers around Boston to bid for Steward's business. And wouldn't you know, Massachusetts General, the big partner of Partners, offered up a combination of services and price, and won the Steward contract. (This is a healthy development. It gives the big hospital more of the specialty work it feasts on. And because it had to offer lower rates to win the competitive bid, it should prod Partners toward improving efficiency and cutting costs.)

De la Torre, for his part, has a strategy for Steward that sounds like a business school case study. He has added new technology. (Disclosure: Steward is an athenahealth client, and as we'll see in chapter 9, it gets its data services for a fraction of what Partners spends.) He has also hacked out overhead, lightening the heavy hand of administration. Part of the trick is to consolidate other operations, such as finance, purchasing, and human resources, so that each hospital doesn't have to run those departments on its own. The viability of its model is no sure thing. But it's a valuable disrupter.

That alone represents progress. A lower-cost provider is carving out the commodity work that shouldn't take place in expensive research hospitals. At the same time, it's giving a research hospital the specialty work it excels at, but at lower rates. What's more, the Steward model makes money by working to keep patients healthy outside the hospital. Its business plan does not revolve around itemized pages of overpriced bandages, X-rays, and consultations. At the same time, a certain amount of shopping is happening—among doctors and corporate executives, though not yet patients. The market is starting to do its work.

But the health care ecosystem is so much broader and deeper than Partners and Steward. They both run hospitals, after all. And just the way Steward is trying to carve out a living from the research hospitals, other more agile players are angling to feed on inefficiencies at community hospitals. I'll move on to them in the next chapter.

First, though, I'd like to return to that earlier discussion I had with the folks at the pediatric hospital, when I told them to buy a jet. Their biggest problem is that most of their potential customers, fortunately, never need the hospital. Most of us are healthy for most of our days. Now it is true that all of us die, and a great number of us will suffer grave illnesses at one point or another, usually as we approach death. So if you add up everybody's sickest month or two on earth, a great many of us need hospitals. But only about 1 percent of us need them at one time. Another 8 percent of us have chronic ailments and are usually ill-served by hospital emergency rooms. The rest of us are healthy and avoid hospitals.

The hospitals' challenge, similar in a way to the insurance industry's, is to lasso in the huge portion of the population that doesn't need them—at least not yet. Steward looks to accomplish this by means of risk contracts. With these, it hopes to make a profit on healthy customers and spend a portion of it on sick ones. Big research hospitals like Partners are preparing for a shift in this model by hiring doctors and laying claim to as many of their patients as possible. In the meantime, though, they're monetizing this customer base by selling them high-priced tests and procedures.

In a market economy, however, as prices become transparent and shoppers entertain more choices, the big hospitals will increasingly struggle to draw business from the 99 percent of us that aren't terribly ill. This is why, I predict, many hospitals will fail in the coming years.

This does not mean that tertiary medical centers will disappear. Many of them will survive, and that's a good thing, because we need their excellence. But to make the transition, they will have to shift their strategy. As I was explaining to the directors of the pediatric hospital, each research hospital will have to expand its market share not by bringing in more healthy people, but by reaching across geography to find more sick ones. That 1 percent of the population is actually huge, more than three million people. And if a research hospital with a niche specialty can lay claim even to 0.05 percent of them, that would be more than fifteen hundred patients, all of them with great needs that bring in loads of revenue. Even more important, the people at the hospital would be carrying out great and heroic work, rescuing lives. That's what attracted them to medicine in the first place. It has to be a lot more fulfilling than shuttling through patients for overpriced MRIs and colonoscopies.

This specialization is already happening. Consider the case of Steve Jobs, the iconic co-founder of Apple Inc. In 2009, he was fighting pancreatic cancer and desperately needed a liver transplant. A billionaire, Jobs had the wherewithal to shop. Traveling on a private jet, he visited hospitals around the country and got himself on various liver transplant waiting lists. Then one day in June of that year, he got the call that Methodist University Hospital in Memphis had access to the liver of a young car-crash victim. Jobs was at the top of the transplant list. The donor's blood was a match. The liver would remain viable for only four hours. But that was enough time for Jobs to fly from California to Memphis. The transplant gave him another two years of life.

While most of us aren't in a position to hop into a private jet at a moment's notice, Jobs's story shows a national market taking shape. The Memphis hospital had an edge over the hospitals near Jobs's home in Palo Alto, California. As he later explained, Methodist had a better supply/demand ratio of livers. Other hospitals with an edge in one specialty or another can increasingly market to a national or international market. In fact, they'll have to.

Cleveland Clinic, one of the nation's preeminent cardiology centers, is taking steps to become a player in this national market. In 2012, the hospital signed an agreement with Lowes, the home-improvement store. It established Cleveland Clinic as the destination for any of Lowes' 228,000 employees and their dependents requiring heart surgery—assuming they're healthy enough to travel. The deal covers travel and lodging for patients and one companion. It provides world-class health care to Lowes employees, and because Lowes is providing bulk business, the company gets the care for a 25 percent discount.

What's not to like? Cleveland Clinic turns even more toward the heart, hiring more cardiologists, carrying out more research, extending its lead. Others will take the lead in other areas. Increasingly, hospitals are going to be evaluating their strengths this way, piece by piece, as they seek their foothold in the future. They'll face tough choices regarding what to jettison and what to build on.

This planning will be difficult, because the economics of their business will be in flux. Prices for the complicated treatments they focus on, for example, are likely to drop. After all, they'll be appealing to shoppers in superregional markets, and not monopolizing the locals. At the same time, though, they will be utilizing their assets much more efficiently, which will drive down costs. Profit per patient should be much higher than it is with the status quo—a smattering of tertiary cases supported by high fees on everything else.

The dynamics in this coming market economy also promise to be entirely different. Hospitals and medical centers will compete not only for each patient, but for each part of that patient's treatment. Imagine a woman in the Houston suburb of Katy, Texas, who has cancer. Fortunately for her, she gets to go to M. D. Anderson, the top-rated cancer center in the country. It's about forty minutes east on I-10.

Now what is it that makes M. D. Anderson Cancer Center great? I'd say it's the highly experienced doctors who study the form, size, chemistry, and behavior of her cancer, diagnose it, and come up with a customized treatment schedule. Ideally, a doctor consults closely with her and her family about the diagnosis and the various options, and then spells out a regime, perhaps including radiation and chemotherapy. M. D. Anderson's expertise in such cases can and does save lives.

With her customized plan in hand, this woman could drive downtown twice a week for the prescribed treatments. But most days she won't see her doctor. And it's not like the brilliant specialists at M. D. Anderson created the chemical that's flowing into her body. The chemo drip is no different from what she'd get a half mile from her house, in Katy. The people administering the treatment don't have a special Houston technique. In fact, some of them probably commute from places like Katy. So what's the advantage of getting treatments at the country's top-ranked cancer center? It's minimal at best, and perhaps negative if the long commute complicates her life. In the best of cases, she might even get a rebate—cash in the pocket—for taking this treatment at a nearby clinic.

What's more, her local options are sure to expand. I recently saw the news that Schnucks, a midwestern grocery chain, is opening its first infusion center. That means that people can get medicine through a needle or catheter, whether for cancer, multiple sclerosis, or Crohn's disease, while picking up frozen lima beans or a half gallon of milk. The parking is sure to be a lot easier than at the university hospital downtown. And Schnucks will even be administering some of the services right in the patients' homes.

Facing this scenario, the challenge for hospitals like M. D. Anderson is to figure out how to leverage its expertise while shedding its lucrative commodity business. Telemedicine might be part of the answer. Jets will no doubt play a part.

These are the dilemmas hospitals will be grappling with as the marketplace reaches their stately doors. Many of them, I'm betting, will fail the test and fold.

Up to this point, you might take me for a hater of hospitals. Nothing could be further from the truth. I remember being in room 4 of Charity Hospital in New Orleans and having my hand, literally, on a beating human heart. The intense concentration of human brilliance and miraculous machines in hospitals inspires awe and gratitude. I even love the rush of all those smart and caring people hurrying around in their scrubs, carrying beepers. But these institutions have to specialize. And I won't shed any tears for those that are left behind as the market shifts. In fact, if half of the hospitals disappear, it will just mean that competitors are doing a better job.

What kind of competitors? I call them the crazy ones.

CHAPTER SIX

■

The Crazy Ones

The United States boasts a health care elite that can match that of any country on earth. It features leaders of powerful university hospitals, world-class surgeons, and brilliant researchers filing patents every day for new drugs and devices. Those are today's titans. But the status quo they work to preserve is unlikely to keep them on top.

Tomorrow's titans are laboring on the periphery. They're all but invisible to the policy crowd in Washington. Few of them hire lobbyists. They don't attend the black-tie fund-raisers at the Kennedy Center. These people are rough-hewn and break the old rules. And they're engaged in radical and unusual behavior. They're busy making money in health care by building something new and appealing to shoppers. For me, they're much like the wildcatters who stormed to fortunes in oil, and the hackers, like the Steve Jobs, who outraced the staid leaders of technology and helped to build a new information economy. These people, to quote Apple's iconic 1984 commercial, are the "crazy ones."

These crazy ones are committed to health and their patients, of course, but I've noticed that most of them don't mind talking about money. It's a subject that is broached only in hushed tones and inscrutable bills in the great research hospitals. But the entrepreneurs I'm talking about celebrate their earnings.

Here's a case in point. One spring day I place a call from my office in Watertown, Massachusetts, to the Boca Raton, Florida, office of Kenneth A. Konsker. He's an obstetrician who had the brilliant idea of doing what our Athena Women's Health team attempted in San Diego all those years ago: to build a great business around delivering babies. Sure, there are some notable differences between our old company and what Konsker and his partner, John Briggs, cooked up in Florida. The most important, by far, is that their company, Florida Woman Care, is growing wildly, while ours grew fast but went broke.

Konsker answers the phone. To put this conversation in perspective, I'm the CEO of a publicly traded company with more than fifty thousand providers as customers. Konsker is a customer. "*Jonny!*" he shouts with a voice straight from New York. Within seconds, he is telling me that he appreciates my offer to send a jet to Boca Raton to ferry him to our users' conference on the coast of Maine. I have made no such offer.

"It'll be just fantastic," he says, thanking me again.

I laugh and attempt to change the subject. But he keeps talking about how much he's looking forward to the sessions in Maine, which of course he cannot get to without the jet. At this point, he is joined by Briggs, who quickly picks up the theme. He too is grateful for the ride.

It's around this point that I realize that despite all the joking, we're actually *negotiating*. There's no way I'm going to spend all that money to ferry a couple of clients the entire length of the Atlantic coast and back again. But saying no consumes a bit of negotiating capital. It raises the pressure, ever so slightly, to say yes to something. This is the game they play. It's a different approach from, say, the Mayo Clinic's.

We move on to talk about something else they're all too happy to discuss: money. Florida Woman just got a round of venture funding, Konsker says. "We got a terrific valuation. Forty-six million!"

Just five years ago, Konsker and Briggs were running their own obstetrics practices, and now they have an enterprise worth $46 million. How did that happen? Well, they tapped into a monster growth market that we might as well call "stuff hospitals suck at." This is the market that will fuel the rebirth of a more efficient and caring health care industry. The growth can be explosive, because the room for improvement is breathtakingly vast. In just five years, Konsker and Briggs have put together a network that accounts for one out of four births in Florida. And with their new venture funding, they're moving to expand nationally. "We're blowing out North Carolina," Konsker tells me.

In the broad ecosystem of health care, community hospitals like Steward's feast on the high prices, inefficiencies, and indifferent service of research hospitals, like Partners. But that's just the beginning of the struggle. Outfits like Florida Woman form a second ring of providers. They build thriving businesses at the expense of hospitals large and small. And other start-ups will no doubt probe the weaknesses of Florida Woman (provided that the incumbents and their legislative protectors don't erect more legal and regulatory barriers).

These insurgents, naturally, are tiny compared to the towering incumbents. While Konsker and Briggs no doubt feel flush with their new funding, Partners HealthCare takes in more than five times their valuation, or $269 million, in annual gifts and donations! Its revenue tops $9 billion per year—more than Florida Woman's $46 million every two days. If you picture this as a race, Partners, Sloan Kettering, Cleveland Clinic, Johns Hopkins, Mayo, and the others line up with gleaming chariots hitched to Thoroughbreds. But their chariots are attached to rails, like the ones at Disney World. They're big and powerful, but they can't steer. By comparison, the crazy ones, like Florida Woman, operate tiny toys on matchbox wheels pulled by gerbils. They're easy to dismiss, just as IBM and the others did when confronted by upstarts like Apple. My money, though, is on the gerbils. In fact, the business model of our company, athenahealth, is built upon equipping them with affordable information services so that they can take on the giants.

The business proposition that led to Florida Woman was simple as could be. Konsker, who grew up on Long Island, was a resident in the early 1990s at Mount Sinai, a research giant in New York City. He had a hand in the business side as the hospital worked to create its ob-gyn arm. He understood billing and coding, and he saw that the hospital was groaning under punishing overhead expenses. The model left lots of room for entrepreneurs. He moved to Florida and became the only ob-gyn doctor at a multispecialty group.

There he developed a strikingly effective business plan. It was centered on moving minimally invasive gynecology procedures from the hospital to an office setting. He went to the insurance providers with data showing that this change could cut the cost of the procedure by more than half. That got their attention.

Then he got really creative. He offered to teach other ob-gyn doctors best practices for performing the same procedures—as long as they joined the management service he was building with Briggs. Soon dozens of doctors in Florida were signing up. Together they had greater buying power to negotiate rates with commercial players. And they could get even lower rates for their back-office services I was selling them.

Briggs followed a similar path. He too grew up in New York, in Queens. He joined a small group in Florida as soon as he got out of med school, at age twenty-nine. But when he met up with Konsker he saw the business model that became Florida Woman Care. In addition to sharing technology, human resources, and marketing, the doctors would share knowledge, developing best practices to drive down costs, raise customer satisfaction, and deliver the highest percentage possible of healthy babies. A baby born in an FWC practice is 50 percent less likely than average to wind up in an intensive care unit. This is terrific for the bottom line but, far more important, better for the babies.

FWC offered doctors more freedom than the hospitals. The doctors could be their own bosses. And they had a good chance to earn more money while charging the patients less. For example, a tubal ligation performed in the hospital costs about $8,000, but performed in one of their offices may cost only $4,000, Konsker tells me. "Now, in the office it's less money, but we keep it all!" FWC can gain market share by charging less than hospitals. While most insurance companies don't bother shopping for lower costs (because they're loathe to alienate the expensive hospitals they need), they're also not dumb. So they nudge women toward Florida Woman. "The only one who loses," Konsker tells me, "is the hospital. And who cares?"

This model clearly appeals to doctors. The practice started out in 2008, with three doctors. By 2013, it had grown to 312 physicians and another 130 midlevel practices. By this point, Florida Woman has the Sunshine State pretty well covered.

This growth is happening for a very simple reason: In the developing health care economy, doctors have more power than hospitals. They haven't always known this. As I mentioned in the last chapter, many doctors still view the hospitals as a safe haven, and thousands are selling them their practices. But in a market focused on establishing long-term relations with patients, doctors hold the cards. This is especially true of primary care doctors, whose perceived value (and pay) has been plummeting since the days of television's *Marcus Welby, M.D.* These doctors control the spending on their patients. Hospitals do not. Doctors have the data and the communication links with patients, and increasingly the good ones will be transitioning into the role of a coach. Outside of urgent care and illness, which affect a small fraction of the population, what do they need hospitals for?

Pipelines of patients represent a lifeline for all kinds of health care businesses. In 2012, DaVita Inc., a dialysis company, paid $4.42 billion in cash and stocks for HealthCare Partners, a grouping of medical practices in the western United States with nearly seven hundred thousand patients. That comes to $6,000 per patient. Only a fraction of them will need dialysis, but as fee for service fades away, the growing business will be in managing patient populations.

A big piece of managing a patient population, of course, is obstetrics. Childbirth is by far the most expensive procedure most women undergo before reaching Medicare age, and it ties into family health. The next big opportunity, as Konsker and Briggs see it, is to sign risk contracts to cover women throughout their pregnancy, from the moment the stripe turns blue on the pregnancy test to the birth of the baby. Mastering this will require lots of data analysis, figuring out which tests and procedures lead to the best results and which are a waste of money. But the doctors will also need to study human behavior. Since a doctor sees a patient for only a minuscule fraction of the pregnancy, much of the success will be up to the woman: the choices she makes about diet, sleep, drinking, stress management, and exercise, and her awareness when things don't feel right. All of this will require testing. Which instructions work? Do e-mail reminders wind up in spam folders? Are diagrams too simple for college graduates? It will require research, but the process in Florida and elsewhere should lead to healthier pregnancies and babies—and lower costs. Konsker sees these episodic risk contracts growing at 5 to 10 percent in Florida in coming years. He believes they are going to save 30 to 40 percent of the total spend by taking on global risk. "That's the exciting opportunity," he says.

Naturally, they're going to be battling hospitals. As the fee structures move toward what providers do *for* their patients, and not *to* them, hospitals will need their share of lives to care for. That's why they've been madly hiring doctors and buying practices, and why the value of the family doctor is skyrocketing. Increasingly, fast-growing practices like FWC pose a mortal threat. Konsker doesn't mince words. He says hospitals have "duped" physicians for years. He says that he tells fellow MDs: "They're not your friends. They're your adversaries." And as hospitals grow more desperate to fill their beds and cover their costs, "It's going to get worse."

We end the call with Konsker, and I compare booming Florida Woman with our failed birthing venture in San Diego. They have a lot in common, both of them focusing on best practices, efficiency, technology—and the emphasis on the caregiver's relationship with the patient. But while we aimed to reinvent birthing from the get-go, with episodic risk sharing, they went right for the money. Now that they have a strong market position, they're positioning themselves to pull off our original dream: guiding patients through the entire pregnancy, and optimizing it in the process.

One advantage Konsker and Briggs have, of course, is that athenahealth is handling all of the billing and back office busywork that helped to sink my business. It's as if we fell into a chasm back then and proceeded to build a bridge that spans it. Now our customers are crossing it, which is hugely satisfying.

But there's another difference, and it's one that makes FWC vulnerable in the health care ecosystem. The whole FWC pitch is focused on doctors helping doctors free themselves from hospitals, deepen interactions with patients, and make more money. But if you remember our business model in San Diego, a crucial piece of it was to reduce the role of doctors. We used midwives, who cost a whole lot less. The idea was to concentrate the valuable attention of doctors on the cases that required their expertise.

For now, FWC is doing fine. There's a huge profit belly in hospitals, with so much waste and overbilling that FWC practices can make money, even with expensive doctors carrying out routine tasks. In markets in which customers are free to shop, competing against big hospitals for routine care is a cinch. But in a vibrant health care market, I'm betting, it's only a matter of time before competitors powered by midwives, medics, and other nondoctor professionals take them on. Then, perhaps, FWC practices will respond by tweaking their model. That's the way healthy markets should work.

It's certainly happening in urgent care. The emergency room is a vital unit in a hospital. Ambulances like the one I drove in New Orleans literally bring in new patients. And many of them, once in the hospital, require care from specialists. Thanks to the emergency room, the hospital often gains control over a patient's care and—to put it in business terms—revenue stream. But should hospitals be treating everything from sprained ankles to cardiac arrest in emergency rooms? Turns out there's lots of room for competitors.

About a decade ago, a physician's assistant in North Carolina named Jason Williams witnessed the tremendous waste in a hospital emergency department. He noticed that 70 percent of the patients used only 10 percent of the enormously expensive equipment in the hospital. And he saw that people like him, with limited medical education, were handling much of the work doctors did at one third the cost. So he started a business offering 70 percent of the service for a fraction of the expense. Think sore throats and kitchen accidents—not strokes. His start-up would offer fast and friendly service at reasonable prices. People would know in advance how big the bill would be: $59, $79, or $99. They wouldn't have to fill out forms on a clipboard time and again, because their records would be electronic. And costs would be lower, in part because physicians' assistants supervised by a handful of doctors would handle 85 percent of the work. He rented a closed-down regional post office near Raleigh, North Carolina, and opened a business called Urgent Care of America. The business, which later became known as FastMed Urgent Care, took off. By 2010, Williams had nine centers and sold it to a group of investors. Now FastMed runs fifty-two centers in North Carolina and Arizona. They are stealing business from slow and expensive hospital ERs and sleepy medical practices with limited hours, and they're doing it by offering urgent services with the spirit and efficiency and profit drive of a Starbucks or a Staples.

I recently talked to John Randazzo, the CEO. This man is a local hospital's nightmare. He and his company are attacking them at their weakest points: convenience, efficiency, and customer service. FastMed sends employees to study customer service at a Ritz Carlton training center. Receptionists and others learn to look the patient in the eye and say their name three times while calling up their records and arranging their care. The service resembles the Genius Bar at the Apple Store, which is precisely the point: Health care should figure out how to provide service and convenience like the rest of the economy.

Focusing on the customer, FastMed sets up practices in underserved areas. It analyzes fifty different elements, from traffic patterns to economic growth, when picking locations for new clinics. The company often sets up in former Hollywood or Blockbuster video offices in strip malls, usually near a Starbucks or a Five Guys burger restaurant. Those retailers developed locations between suburban communities and downtown. But for a medical provider like FastMed, it acts as a cutoff: If your kid needs stitches, do you want to get off in one exit and have easy parking, or drive all the way downtown and look for a space in a crowded hospital lot?

For many people, the local FastMed functions as a primary care doctor. FastMed is equipped to handle 70 percent of emergency room cases. That includes a certain number of people who don't need an emergency room, but don't yet know it. These patients feel symptoms that could be serious, but turn out not to be. FastMed sends them to the hospital for tests on some of the expensive machinery, just in case. But that raises an interesting point. Since FastMed doesn't have fancy diagnostic equipment, it faces fewer legal problems. No one can sue them for not running a precautionary MRI. Hospitals, by contrast, often feel pressure to run expensive tests if only to avoid legal complications—and they make loads of money in the process.

The savings at FastMed over an average emergency department visit are 90 percent. I kid you not. Interestingly, since 90 percent of FastMed's patients have insurance, they don't benefit from the lower prices, but their insurers do. The insured patients come simply for the convenience and the service. Most visits cost $99. (Discounts are available, Randazzo says, for some uninsured patients.) In 2013, FastMed was named the fastest-growing privately owned company in North Carolina. But just imagine how fast it would be growing if more customers were paying out of pocket. Price is FastMed's biggest competitive advantage, and it has barely come into play.

In any case, the company continues to expand, and is spreading into new services. Every inefficiency in the industry, and every overcharged procedure, represents a new opportunity. FastMed is looking to hire dermatologists and link them through the Internet to various clinics. A photo might be all they need to renew a prescription or change medication. "Acne could be a great market for us," Randazzo tells me.

In this new competitive wing of the health care ecosystem, however, Randazzo faces competition for acne, and for plenty of other services as well. Plenty of small and nimble players are spreading around the country. Very similar to FastMed is a West Virginia start-up called MedExpress. It was the brainchild of Frank Alderman, a doctor who grew up near the famous Greenbriar resort. The customer service there impressed him, and he has built a business around getting it into medicine. MedExpress now operates 120 centers in eight states. If your kid needs a physical for summer camp or the soccer team, you make an appointment online and swing by. At MedExpress the posted price is $20. This is marketing with the clarity of Jiffy Lube.

Some of the stiffest competition for FastMed and MedExpress is already coming from behemoths like CVS, Target, and Walgreens. And why not? These giants already have millions of customers. They have their credit cards, their customer loyalty data. They already sell them drugs and medicines. So why not branch into medical services as well?

It's only natural. These companies make their living by optimizing customer services. They figure out how to deliver what shoppers want faster and a dime or a dollar cheaper than their competitors. That is, they're the polar opposite of hospitals. But by putting medical professionals behind the counter, they can carve off a lucrative slice of the hospitals' business. A few years ago, the Walgreens pharmacy chain merely sold medicines. Now, increasingly, it administers them. Of the more than 9 million flu vaccines it sold in 2012, it administered 5.5 million of the injections in its own clinics. These clinics are spreading dramatically, doubling in the last six years to fourteen hundred clinics in 2013. CVS, as I write this, runs about eight hundred MinuteClinics, and is adding about three new locations every week. Unlike doctors' offices, these clinics are often open in the evening and on weekends. Patients know what they're buying, and how much it will cost. A test for a strep throat at CVS, for example, costs $27. The first "hello" at an emergency department costs a crooked multiple of that. What's more, the emergency department serves as the gateway to hospital admissions.

More than 80 percent of unscheduled hospital admissions come through the emergency departments, according to a 2013 report from the American College of Emergency Physicians. And that feeds a wasteful inpatient care industry that, according to a Rand study, consumes 31 percent of what we spend on health care.

I spend lots of time thinking about where we need more newcomers in health care and more innovative start-ups. Every time I see an insane price from a hospital, I run the numbers in my head. For example, Martha Bebinger, a reporter for WBUR in Boston, shopped in 2012 for an MRI. When she finally got someone at Massachusetts General to give her a price—which is no easy thing—she learned that an insured patient would be billed $5,315. I've seen higher and lower numbers, but let's start with that figure. Now say a couple of entrepreneurs wanted to compete in that business (and weren't blocked by the government). They'd rent a machine for about $8,000 a month. Say the room in some suburban office park costs $1,000. The technician costs $5,000 a month, maybe $6,500 if you include vacation, health insurance, and other benefits. Let's add $3,000 for taxes and fees. They could be up and running for about $18,500 a month. Maybe they add another technician, so they can run it twelve hours a day. That's $25,000.

Now assume that since they'll charge a fraction of the going rate, they'll have plenty of business. They can do three images every hour. If they work twelve hours, that's thirty-six per day, or nine hundred every month. According to those numbers, they pay their expenses and break even at $28 per image. If they put up a big sign offering MRIs at $99, they could be rolling in profits—by charging less than 1 percent of the big hospital price. My back-of-the-envelope estimates could be off by 100 percent, and there'd still be enormous room for making money. You could almost conclude that those crazy outliers setting up businesses in health care aren't so crazy after all.

CHAPTER SEVEN

Making Money with Primary Care

One day a few years ago, a woman came to a clinic in Las Vegas. She had been fainting of late, and was understandably worried. The doctor she saw happened to be Rushika Fernandopulle, one of the country's leaders in rethinking and remaking health care. Rushika (whom I always call by his first name, like Ichiro or Elvis) spent a couple of hours with this woman, looking into the medication she took. It turned out that she was on twenty-seven different medicines prescribed by eleven different doctors, most of them specialists. She had seven medications for hypertension alone, four of them the exact same drug.

Rushika asked her how she managed to take all of those pills. She shook her head and said it was impossible for her. Instead she put the medicine into a jar and asked God every day to place the five she should take into her hand. Naturally, if three or four of them turned out to be the same drug, she would have a very bad and dangerous day. And who would she call if she did? Each one of those specialists looked out for a part of her. But clearly no one was caring for the entire person.

That's what Rushika wants to do. As a young doctor, Rushika practiced at Mass General—in the belly of the beast. There he witnessed the wonders performed by the medical elite, and also got his fill of the dysfunctional system that sustained it. At the same time, he was running a health policy program at Harvard. As he tells it, this allowed him to travel around the country, meeting both innovators and stick-in-the-muds, all on Harvard's dime. From this research and his own experience, he concluded that the U.S. health care system simply could not be fixed with tweaks—a conviction he holds to this day. "The system is broken, and most people just sit around and complain about it," he says. "Why don't we just start over?"

The way Rushika sees it, the status quo is fundamentally misaligned. Each of us, on average, spends a little more than half a day per year in a hospital. Yet we pour nearly a third of our health care dollars into inpatient care—five times as much as primary care. This status quo, of course, is already under attack. As we've seen, outfits like Steward, Florida Woman Care, and MedExpress are all munching away happily on hospital business, and making the industry more responsive and efficient as they grow. But their efforts, in a sense, are like organ transplants. They make the pieces work better, but it's still the same body.

Rushika, by contrast, launched a company in 2004, Renaissance Health, with the goal of pushing for an entirely different scheme—changing the payment model, staffing, and technology. Everything. His idea was to turn the industry ratio on its head, and lavish customers with primary care.

The initial challenge he faced, though, was to find health care customers unhappy with the status quo and eager for disruption. At first he tried something that for a very smart guy was a bit stupid. He went to all the big health systems in Boston and told them he needed a lab. Just let me handle one of your practices, he said, and he would figure out a better way to deliver health care.

What exactly, they wanted to know, was he going to fix? They were making money. Maybe he saw a problem, but they didn't.

Clearly, this line wasn't going to work. Rushika needed to find people who were unhappy with the status quo. It was about then that he got a call from a physician named Arnold Milstein. He was a "global thought leader" for Mercer, a consulting firm that advised unions and employers on health benefits. In the early 2000s, Milstein had worked with Unite Here, the union representing hotel and casino workers in Las Vegas. The union had a contract that put aside funds for benefits. Year after year the rank and file were promised that any savings from this fund would underwrite pay hikes. This sounded fine. But as you can imagine, all potential savings were swallowed up by ballooning health care costs. Pay was stuck at an average of $13 per hour. Union members were working poor and getting poorer. Unlike most Americans, they could see in lurid detail how exploding health care costs were emptying their pockets. So in 2003, the union contracted with Milstein.

"I told them," Milstein says, "that doctors are like cars. Some give you forty miles per gallon on health insurance fuel. Some give you ten. We're going to take the bad ones out of the network." In short, Milstein was going to shop on behalf of the workers. He crunched data and calculated an efficiency ranking for doctors in the system. Then he targeted about sixty doctors, or 10 percent of the total, whose billing was egregious, and eliminated them from the program. From that point on, if union members wanted to go to those sixty doctors, they would have to pay out of pocket.

This outraged the doctors. The next day, many of them were picketing hotels and urging workers to call and complain to the union. (Yes, you've read that right: Doctors were picketing the union workers.) Bean counters, they argued, were disrupting the "sacred" relationship between doctors and patients. But in fact, if union members had seen the consequences of the stratospheric invoices on their personal income, they would have fired them themselves.

The benefits soon became clear. Within fifteen months, the union registered a $55 million reduction in health care. Milstein attributes much of it to a salutary effect on the remaining doctors. With someone scrutinizing their bills and ready to take action, they toed the line. Union workers the next year received a pay hike of $1.10.

It wasn't long before Boeing, the airplane manufacturer, contacted Milstein. The company self-insured its workforce and was looking for relief. Health care bills were rising, and these costs were hurting the company's global competitiveness. Milstein soon saw that Boeing presented a more complex problem than the Unite Here union. Fixing it would involve more than ferreting out the most expensive doctors. Instead, the company needed to turn the focus on the most expensive patients. There was a minority of them, about 8 percent of the workforce, that gobbled up massive amounts of health care, well over half of the total expense. This had to change. The only way to do it was to reinvent health care. That's when Milstein called Rushika.

When the two doctors studied Boeing's health care expenditures, they quickly saw that the chronically ill—including employees and family members covered—represented an enormous opportunity. The modern health care system, with its focus on crisis response, simply wasn't (and isn't) designed to satisfy their needs. It was clear from the records that these people, many of them suffering from chronic illnesses, often exacerbated by obesity or mental health issues, were routinely ignored until their symptoms resulted in a crisis. At that point the hospital addressed the problem at immense expense and then sent them home until the crisis returned, which it inevitably did. This pattern continued until they died.

This approach worked magnificently at generating revenue—which was precisely Boeing's problem. The patients' crises often resulted in hospital stays and loads of expensive tests, procedures, and medicines.

But this care did not cure, or even reduce, the intensity of the chronic disease. Hospitals simply weren't built for that work. The chronically ill would come again and again until finally, at death's door, many of them would pass their final days, weeks, even months, in a hospital bed, with ever more expenses cascading, minute by minute, onto the bill. From a budgetary perspective, it was as if a significant portion of the Boeing population was living it up in luxury suites at the Ritz, ordering cases of champagne and tubs of caviar, getting pedicures, permanents, and hot-stone massages, and making off with the terry cloth robes. Boeing, of course, was footing the bill, and I should note that despite the expense, their chronically ill employees and family members were suffering terribly.

Rushika saw that he could save millions for the Boeing system by turning the status quo on its head: His approach would spend money, lots of it, to keep these expensive customers *out* of hospitals. Advanced medicine, he knew, was virtually powerless against most chronic diseases. The most effective and lasting improvements came from changes in lifestyle management. For this, Rushika would focus instead on helping these people make healthier choices.

He proceeded to shower Boeing's chronically ill with health care. He supplemented the doctors on Boeing's plan with case managers and health coaches. They reached out to the patients to help them cope with their ailments. They talked to them about diets, how to shop for healthy food and prepare it, and how to manage stress, ideally with exercise. They coached them to monitor their blood sugar or their blood pressure, or set up reminders to take medicines. This is known as "wraparound" care. The key for the patients was to learn to perceive when troubles were on the horizon, and to respond to them earlier rather than later.

This approach lowered the rate of hospital visits and, most important, improved people's lives. The chronically ill at Boeing were managing their conditions and suffering fewer frightening and painful emergencies. What wasn't to like? It's true that hiring all these health coaches cost a lot of money. But keeping the people out of hospitals saved far more. In the first year, according to an independent academic analysis, Boeing's outlays for the target population were down by 20 percent compared to a control group. And the target group had higher customer satisfaction, better clinical outcomes, and missed workdays half as often.

Through this process, Rushika and his team were learning important lessons about coaching. The key was not simply to have the right information for the patients or to contact them at the right times. The chronically ill didn't want or need more authority figures calling them up and knocking on their door. No, coaches had to learn how to engage with patients and convince them that they were working together. The coach should arrive with more questions than answers, because the key was to understand the habits and peculiarities of each person's life, and how best to adapt them to new routines. This required communication and a knack for different cultures. Humor helped. Significantly, it didn't require a workforce of health care know-it-alls. In fact, high school graduates with the right skills could be trained to do the work and collect the relevant data. This meant that the potential labor pool was large and relatively cheap.

Despite the successes, many of the doctors weren't happy. Sure, the results were impressive for the target group. But once they saw how well it worked, it seemed unfair to restrict the benefits to only 8 percent of their patients. Many of the other employees would benefit from the coaching, but weren't expensive enough to qualify for it. This, Rushika says, made some of the doctors feel bad. It was as if patients had to be really sick to get the kind of care everyone deserved. (This fact might get lost or ignored in my critique of the health care system, but of the fifty thousand providers I work for, the vast majority are aching to do great and meaningful work. And they'd flock to a system that provided more opportunities for it—provided they didn't have to take a big pay cut.)

Rushika's Renaissance Health went on to work with a host of different clients, for companies and unions. But Renaissance never had complete control of the process. Its mandate, after all, was to cut costs and improve services, but to leave intact certain parts of each program. This usually meant leaving relatively healthy people with the status quo. In short, the consultants couldn't just blow it up and start over, which was precisely what Rushika wanted to do.

He was thinking about widening the focus of the program. If the wraparound method worked for the chronically ill, why not use it for everyone? No doubt the math was different. While the enormous expenses of the chronically ill could underwrite large teams of coaches knocking on doors, the savings for relatively healthy people wouldn't be nearly as large. Most people, fortunately, go for years on end without donning a hospital gown and plastic bracelet. But those people wouldn't require as much coaching, either. And maybe with a little coaching, and unfettered access to primary care, they'd live better and longer, and cost even less. Rushika didn't know the answer, but he wanted to experiment.

For this he needed to create a new type of health care provider. So just down the road from me, in Cambridge, he founded Iora Health. After its first two years, Iora had four practices up and running, each one offering a new type of health services to a specific population. In Las Vegas it was hotel and casino workers, in New York City a union of freelancers.

In each practice, the customer chooses a doctor and a coach within the system. These are Iora employees. They don't benefit from giving marginal tests and procedures, nor do they profit from savings if they withhold them. This keeps the focus on the patient's health. When customers have serious problems, they are sent to specialists in the network. But the goal is to keep their patients healthy. To this end, customers can visit or call or e-mail their primary care doctors as often as they want—at no additional charge. The idea, Rushika says, is that people should not be discouraged in any way from primary care. This is expensive, without a doubt, especially when hypochondriacs get into the game. But if the outlay on primary care eliminates even a small percentage of hospitalizations, it can pay for itself.

Patients in the Iora system not only have a right to see their medical records, but can also take their own notes during meetings and have them included in the file. That's a small innovation. Bigger ones include a host of supporting services. Iora offers yoga, cooking classes, ergonomics assistance, meditation, and acupuncture. The goal, clearly, is not just to respond to illnesses, but to promote healthier lives.

Does acupuncture pay for itself? Do cooking classes? It's early still, and Iora is an experiment. At this point, Rushika says, the business opportunity for Iora remains in the chronically ill fraction of the population. That's where the money is.

Yoga and cooking classes sound great, of course. But they tend to draw customers who are already healthy. Many of them already pay for such things. Giving yoga to these people as a health care benefit may not generate significant savings. Then again, in the kind of health shopping system I'm pushing for, healthy people would be free to insure themselves only for catastrophes, if they chose, which would lower their insurance premiums, freeing up money for yoga classes and nicotine patches.

I love Iora. But it has one quirk that confounds me: Rushika has a tech team writing custom code. In other words, he is running what amounts to a software start-up within his company, just the way we did in the 1990s.

Now, the way I look it, tech companies like ours hire legions of coders so that outfits like Iora can focus on the patient care that they do best. But this is where our difference gets a bit personal.

Rushika, it turns out, sees our company as an establishment tool. In his eyes, I work for The Man. He's got the same righteous rage that I have for Mass General. I can see it in his eyes. But in his view, my company is aligned with the enemy.

"We need a completely different staffing model, and different IT," he says. "The systems out there, including athenahealth's, are built to record and bill codes. This coding stuff has gotten in the way of good care."

In other words, we help our customers make money from the dysfunctional status quo. They keep better records and code more efficiently for their procedures, and that way they help themselves to their share of the $2.7 trillion health care gusher. They succeed where our San Diego birthing start-up failed. Guilty as charged.

I should add that there are no codes to bill for the kind of work that most of his frontline caregivers provide. They are not licensed practitioners. And even though they are perfect for the work they do, no ordinary health plan will reimburse for such services.

Still, if Rushika's ideas take root, I'm betting the big impact will come as more companies, including ours, figure out how to incorporate them into effective and profitable business models, even as they feed off the status quo.

This is already happening. Consider the case of Dr. Dean Ornish. Decades ago, he was a pioneer in studying and promoting lifestyle changes to fight off illnesses, from heart disease to prostate cancer. In the early nineties, he was President Bill Clinton's physician. First Lady Hillary Clinton had him work with White House chefs to prepare healthier fare for the first family and their guests. Now he heads the Preventive Medicine Research Institute, just across the Golden Gate from San Francisco. This is a guy who finds loads of common ground with Rushika.

He's also interested in making a buck. He recently joined forces with a company called Healthways to offer comprehensive lifestyle behavior regimes as treatment for chronic diseases. This regime calls for a healthy diet—fruits, vegetables, and whole grains—along with moderate exercise and stress management. It even includes group therapy and sex counseling. That might not sound revolutionary. You could walk down almost any street from Portland, Oregon, to Portland, Maine, and find people selling similar services. What sets the Ornish program apart is that he has a code, a Medicare code. This means that doctors can prescribe his regime and patients can get reimbursed. With his new venture, Dean Ornish has his hand in the health care honey jar.

Is this bad? Well, the entire payment system is a hideous mess. There are codes for every conceivable drug that addresses heart disease or hypertension, but no codes for fixing those conditions. The fact is that our life choices make a far bigger impact on our health than the prescriptions we pick up at Walgreens. Most of those drugs treat symptoms, but not the disease.

Some might object that implementing change in our eating habits or exercise routines isn't equivalent to taking medicine. But look at the positive side. Ornish is offering care, like Iora's, that focuses on health and leads people away from surgery and drugs. That's wonderful. We have to get it through our heads that health care is not always about treating illness, that only a small fraction of health care has anything to do with hospitals. Ornish helps to steer us in that direction. What's more, if his regime proves successful, it will outlive the rotten payment system, which is unsustainable. In time, doctors running populations on risk contracts might simply direct their chronically ill toward lifestyle management because it works better. By using software analytics, they'll be able to evaluate the effectiveness of these various therapies, sifting out the hype and zeroing in on value. If doctors like Dean Ornish make millions in the process, I'm cheering them on. Their success will serve to draw in more entrepreneurs, who will compete with them, and maybe even supplant them, in a race to improve our health and, at the same time, make money.

CHAPTER EIGHT

The Medical Home in the Woods

On a summer day in the mid-1970s, a young doctor from Yale paddled a canoe through the pristine waters of the Adirondack Mountains. His name was John Rugge. He and a friend, James West Davidson, had a contract to write a book about wilderness canoeing. The area suited Rugge. The canoeing was excellent, and he had family nearby.

Rugge soon learned that a doctor and receptionist in the remote village of Chestertown had fallen in love and abruptly left the community. One thing led to another, and before long, Rugge's summer canoeing gig had morphed into a full-time job as medical director at the Chestertown practice. From a paddler's perspective, Chestertown looked promising. It was some eighty miles north of Albany and right between Loon Lake and the Scroon River.

There was also a growing need for health care. Three decades earlier, the northern Adirondacks had welcomed a slew of doctors fleeing Hitler's Europe. These doctors settled in the small villages scattered throughout the region and provided a vital service. But by the mid-seventies, they were retiring. The immense area was turning into what Rugge calls a "medical vacuum." Rugge, who went to divinity school before studying medicine, already had a clear sense of mission. In the

Adirondacks he found a job to hitch it to. Since then, he has spent four decades using every tool at hand—vision, ingenuity, salesmanship, and political connections, to name four—to fill that vacuum in the headwaters of the Hudson.

If you listen to John Rugge tell his story, he appears to be an unlikely hero for this book. At first glance, he's nothing like the Florida obstetricians, Dr. Konsker and Dr. Briggs, who are building a profitable birthing empire in the South. He couldn't be more different from Steward's Ralph de la Torre, who feeds on the pendulous profit belly of Massachusetts General. It's true that Rugge shares a sense of mission with Rushika Fernandopulle, and for that matter with the other entrepreneurs. They all want to improve the industry. But for Rugge, the money flowing into Hudson Headwaters simply funds the mission. And he uses it to extend a version of Rushika's vision to a large and scattered population.

Rugge runs a nonprofit. I'm not talking about nonprofits like the research hospitals, many of which actually make good money. Rugge's nonprofit, Hudson Headwaters, is the real thing. He has to scrape together money to provide medical services for more than seventy thousand far-flung people in the rural north. And to do this, he doesn't hesitate to hit up the government—yes, the same government I've been railing against for the last several chapters. In the 1970s, he and his colleagues landed government grants to fund medical cooperatives, each one at least half owned by the communities. When the group runs into financial trouble or needs a break, Rugge doesn't hesitate to put in a call to the senior senator from New York, Charles Schumer, who is one of his biggest fans.

As you can probably tell by now, a socialistic nonprofit grouping of community health centers is not my template for the future. I usually view nonprofit clinics as well meaning, but blind to the realities of efficiency and market forces. I lean toward a brand-managed capitalist approach. And I think it's fair to say that John Rugge can find my approach a bit jarring.

From Rugge's perspective, I might as well have dropped in from a different planet. He views health care more as a utility than a competitive market and says that "justice" demands more public oversight than other markets. I'm sure we disagree on how much. I would bet that we don't often pull the same lever in the voting booth. But we're both focused on the same mission: getting health care to work better. From my perspective, the more smart people out there working to fix this problem, the better. Rugge is an innovator.

He's also an entrepreneur. In the early days, the Hudson Headwaters cooperatives operated only in the remote towns and villages of the upper Adirondacks. But with time Rugge realized that the business needed more scale, so it extended into the more populated area around Glens Falls, a larger town an hour north of Albany. With time, Hudson Headwaters became the dominant player in the region.

It provided excellent care, but struggled as a business. In fact, the enterprise grappled with the same problems our birthing start-up had faced in San Diego a decade earlier. Patient records and billing were tangled up in computer programs and filing cabinets, and the company had trouble getting paid. "In every metric, our business administration was toast," recalls George Purdue, who arrived as the chief information officer in 2002. The net collection rate, he says, was in the low eighties. In other words, nearly 20 percent of bills went unpaid. A lot of companies in that situation simply look for a way to squeeze more money out of the 80 percent who pay. The other approach would be to overhaul the administration, a move that would create pain and resistance, with no guarantee that it would succeed. Hudson Headwaters, like so many companies in the same bind, muddled along, or at least tried to. After one payroll in 2007, Purdue recalls, they had only $1,500 left in the bank account.

At that point, there was no choice but to take action. They enlisted our services, and soon we were following the trail of bills, figuring out which services were most effective and efficient, and sharing best practices through the network. My point is not that our service turned Hudson Headwaters around. Instead, it's about how an innovative enterprise learned to focus on information and turn data from a liability into a powerful tool, and then transformed its business and expanded its mission. For traditional companies, this type of turnaround feeds profits. Hudson Headwaters, though, used its dramatic gains in efficiency to fund itself and fulfill its mission. It's doing such great work, in fact, that it risks putting the local hospital out of business.

Early on a frosty fall morning, ten people make their way into a conference room in the Queensbury, New York, offices of Hudson Headwaters. Most are holding steaming cups of coffee. This group includes doctors, nurses, managers, administrators, and a tech guy. For the last couple of years, new streams of data have poured into Hudson Headwaters. They show how the company handles more than seventy thousand patients, and they say something about the results. This group's job is to figure out how to use that data to optimize the workflows and improve the health of the entire population.

A family doctor named Tucker Slingerland is running the meeting. But he was on duty last night at the Glens Falls hospital, and is hunched over his cell phone giving updates about one of his patients to a nurse on the other end of the line. The call ends, and the group looks at a computer dashboard beamed on the wall. It shows how the sixteen health centers are dealing with 213 cases of diabetes in the network.

Some of the centers appear to manage them better than others, judging by their rates of retinal screenings, foot exams, blood tests, and other metrics. Those ones are marked in green. Others are in yellow. (None is in red, thankfully.) What do the yellows have to do to raise their performance? "We look at the health centers that are standing out," Slingerland says, "and see how they're doing it."

They move on to figures about mammograms and pap smears. Instead of looking at the population that's had the tests, maybe they should isolate the group that hasn't had them in two years and reach out to them. Is e-mail the best approach? A phone call? Text messages? They'll have to experiment. In some cases they manage to tiptoe around the antikickback law and give patients a $50 gift card to get the exams. Possible performance reimbursements from Medicare Advantage would more than make up the difference.

Then they focus on one center where the mammogram/pap smear numbers are lagging far behind the others. Could that just be a coincidence? Cyndi Nassivera-Reynolds, the vice president for transformation, pipes up. It turns out that all caregivers in that center are males, she says. That raises questions. Should men be taught how to counsel their patients about such things? Or would it be simpler just to get a woman in there? In the short run, it's probably easier and cheaper to work with the men, and see if the numbers move up.

One of the challenges, especially in a rural district, is to bring in people for tests they don't feel they need. Glaucoma is a good example. The ocular disorder leads to a dangerous buildup of fluids in the eye, and it accounts for about one tenth of the blindness in the United States. It's fairly easy to test for. The doctor just drips anesthesia on the eyeball and then presses down on it with a machine that gauges the pressure. Glaucoma, though, affects only about 1 percent of the adult population. That raises issues for health population efforts. Will ninety-nine out of a hundred people who come in for the test go back home muttering about wasted time? Will this make them less likely to pay attention to the next call, for a flu shot or blood pressure screening? Maybe. So is there some way to isolate the patients with a family history of glaucoma? It's not in the data yet. But eventually it will be.

In these early days of population management, most of the data analysis compares the workflow at the health centers to best practices at the national level. With time, though, care management teams will have more information to close the loop, gauging the effectiveness of their interventions. In the recent past, the sixteen centers all had their own methods, each one guided by the preferences and experience of its team, and each producing its own paper trail. With this new data, all of the centers operate as a single networked laboratory. Each new stream of information raises new questions, and new possibilities for analysis and optimization.

Since implementing the new data network, Dr. Rugge and his team are running a much tighter ship. The bank balance has risen from $1,500 in those bleak days of 2007 to several million dollars. But from Rugge's perspective, solvency serves only one end: to carry out the health care mission. And with the right technology, he and his team can expand it.

It was this idea that led Hudson Headwaters to pursue a new plan. In 2009, while his health centers were still getting used to our cloud-based platform, Rugge saw that this plunge into digital technology could position the enterprise for the next generation of medical care—and a mother lode of new grant financing. Unlike many other providers, he was in a position to carry out e-prescriptions, to share data with patients, and to use evidence-based standards to cut costs and improve results. In short, Hudson Headwaters could be a model citizen for health care 2.0, as the technocrats in Washington and Albany envisioned it. Rugge played every card in his deck, every political contact he could find, even business executives who vacationed in the area, to establish Hudson Headwaters as a pilot for a program called Medical Home.

This program, financed in part by Medicare and Medicaid, along with a slew of state agencies and insurance companies, provides more resources for primary care. The idea is similar to Rushika Fernandopulle's operation at Iora. Hudson Headwaters hires more primary doctors and coaches, organizes them into care teams, and unleashes them on the customers most likely to visit hospitals. Much like Iora, these coaches get to know the patients, their lives, and their ailments. They work on diet and exercise, and they come up with ways to get them to take the right meds at the right time.

Hudson Headwaters also screens the population for depression and mental disease, which is a central (and widely ignored) source not only of pain and distress, but also of self-destructive habits and chronic disease. In addressing mental health, Dr. Rugge positions his rural network at the vanguard of health care. After all, trying to battle obesity, alcoholism, drug abuse, and dozens of other health scourges without addressing mental health is akin to pushing higher education without tackling illiteracy.

One interesting aspect of the more personal care in the Medical Home project, Rugge and his team have discovered, is that it exposes problems that before weren't even visible. Nassivera-Reynolds gives an example. In 2011, patients with chronic ailments, such as congestive heart failure and pulmonary disease, went in and out of the hospital at Glens Falls at an alarming rate. Nearly 20 percent of them were back within a month. The biggest problem was that they didn't take the right medicines. In health care parlance, they didn't "adhere to medications." This much was known.

The Medical Home coaches began to visit these people in their homes, and they noticed a discrepancy. The patients weren't bringing home from the hospital the same medicines that had been prescribed. After some research, it became clear that the nursing staff was putting together packets for the patients from old medication lists. "It was a work flow issue," says Nassivera-Reynolds. Fixing it, along with the coaching of the chronically ill patients, has brought down the readmission rate by more than half, to 7.8 percent.

Sometimes the amount of hand-holding in the Medical Home program feels like a nanny state on steroids. And I have to admit that it sets off all sorts of alarms in my free-market mind. Nassivera-Reynolds tells about a man in his early fifties who went to the emergency room complaining of numbness in his foot. He didn't get much help there. A bit later, a friend of his died of diabetes. This prompted him to stop by a Hudson Headwaters health center in Glens Falls. They tested him and found his blood sugar in the stratosphere, and sky-high cholesterol to boot. So they sent him to a podiatrist for his feet and coached him on how to administer insulin.

Then the Hudson Headwaters team started looking at this man's life. He was unemployed and had no car, but wanted to work as a security guard. They found him classes, and transport to the classes. Now, says Nassivera-Reynolds, he's employed, and dealing constructively with his health issues.

It's an ideal outcome for him. And it's great for all of us, not just because we care about him, but also because he stays out of the hospital. And that's a big point: Hospital care is so ridiculously expensive that avoiding that expense can underwrite personal care for millions of Americans—no matter how it's financed.

In fact, even in the age of data, there's one great advantage to the medical community keeping in touch with patients: If someone knows you, the doctors don't need to leave as much guesswork to expensive machines. For example, a man comes into the emergency room with a splitting headache or perhaps a burning sensation in the vicinity of the heart. If the caregivers there don't know this person, a worst-case analysis might lead them to give him a series of frightfully expensive tests. Indeed, the use of CT scans and MRIs in hospital emergency departments tripled in the first decade of this century. But if a friend tells doctors that he saw him the night before watching the Bills lose on Monday night football, drowning his sorrows in tequila and wolfing down a heaping plate of Buffalo wings, well, that's valuable context.

No doubt, the human beings in the Medical Home pilot project provide similar insights. And by helping to avoid a few unnecessary MRIs, they can more than justify their pay. In fact, if great numbers of hospitals contract and close shop, as I expect, we should have a surplus of health care workers who in the coming decade can turn their attention to customers in their homes. (Then again, to win these jobs, health care workers will have to learn to focus on customer service, an area where they have some catching up to do.)

As I mentioned earlier, there's one significant downside to the Medical Home project in the upper Adirondacks: It's so effective that hospital admissions are plummeting. And John Rugge is wondering what steps he should take to prop up the local Glens Falls hospital. He believes it provides vital emergency services for the region. And like many hospitals across the country, it's also a major employer. In fact, two of the largest employers all the way up to the Canadian border are a pair of hospitals, in Glens Falls and Plattsburgh.

If the hospitals like the one in Glens Falls were to disappear, Rugge says, "you'd have vast swaths of territory with no hospitals and no emergency rooms." He certainly appreciates, better than just about anyone, the dysfunction of most hospitals in America. But he says they must be fixed, not closed. "We have to understand what they can do well, and then do a fundamental reorganization," he says. "We have to rightsize them." But still, he adds, they're necessary. "If you get a heart attack, you need stenting within hours. We have to protect [the hospital's] margins, too."

My solution, as you might guess, is to let failing institutions fail. I have never met anyone at Glens Falls, but I'll bet the hospital is staffed with dedicated professionals who do the best they can. Some no doubt are brilliant. But they face a structural problem. Since they attempt to do almost everything, they don't get enough practice in most specialties to compete with world-class experts. Their workload forces them to be generalists, and this hurts overall quality. In a sense, they're like high school athletes who play every sport, and even toot the clarinet in the marching band. When those people get into college sports, more often than not they get steamrolled by the focused experts who master one position in one sport twelve months a year. Focus matters.

To be sure, Glens Falls is larger and has more scale than the 1,332 small critical access hospitals across rural America. A 2011 study from the Harvard School of Public Health found that patients in those facilities were more likely than average to die from heart attacks, heart failure, and pneumonia. Midsized hospitals like Glens Falls are better equipped to deal with those common emergencies, but are still hardpressed to compete with the large coronary or oncology units at research hospitals.

Now it's true that not everyone in Glens Falls can be rushed off to a world-class facility five hundred or a thousand miles away. Logistical and economic issues prevent that. And yes, the situation remains problematic for far-flung people in places like Montana or Alaska, where even minimal medical services are often far away. But upstate New York is hardly Montana. Only a fifty-mile drive south from Glens Falls stand two hospitals—St. Peter's and Albany Medical Center. Both are ranked among the top twenty in the state by *U.S. News & World Report*, and each boasts a host of specialties. Glens Falls, according to the same study, has none. So if you're in the Adirondacks and you need treatment for a serious heart or lung problem, or cancer, wouldn't you rather go to the specialists an hour away? (This is not to say, incidentally, that helicoptering patients to Albany is a permanent solution, because those hospitals also run general stores, albeit bigger ones. They too will have to focus on a specialty or two—the sooner, the better.)

I can guess what you're thinking. It might make sense for patients who can plan their care to drive an hour away, but sometimes people need emergency help, and access to the expensive technology at hospitals. That's true. But many residents of the Adirondacks live more than an hour from the hospital at Glens Falls. They would actually be better served if the hospital were replaced by a couple of helicopters that could deliver them straight to Albany (or elsewhere). Fifty helicopter trips a year, or even 150, cost a lot less than running a four-hundred-bed hospital 365 days a year.

I have no doubt that even while traffic is declining at the Glens Falls emergency room, it provides valuable service. But what if Hudson Headwaters created its own emergency unit? I can picture it now, an operation clicking along with trademark efficiency and customer focus, all of it linked to the Hudson Headwaters data system and to Medical Home. I imagine it running in the carcass of the Glens Falls hospital. I see a heliport on the roof and, inside, a vibrant start-up providing focused and cutting-edge service. Maybe I'm getting carried away. But when I think about what John Rugge has built in the four decades since he paddled into the Adirondacks, I want it to expand and reach more people.

PART

THREE

The Future of Technology
in Health Care

CHAPTER NINE

Software Wars

In the spring of 2013, disturbing news arrived from Atlanta. Then came an alarming bulletin from Minneapolis and another from New Haven. It was as if our company, athenahealth, were under attack—and taking losses. New fronts seemed to open with each passing week. Presiding over this crisis were embattled hospital executives looking to consolidate market share and lock in streams of patient referrals. And the tool for this strategy was the software system built by our most powerful competitor, a Wisconsin-based software company called Epic. This process threatened to push us out of entire markets. I viewed it as a grave threat to our company, and I assigned five colleagues to set up a strategy hub. We called it the war room.

Their job was to monitor the battles and come up with a strategy to save our business. You might think that a battle involving software systems, while vital to the companies involved, is merely a sideshow in the larger drama over health care in America. But this confrontation concerns the flow of medical data, and who has access to it. I don't want to overstate this, creating stark polarities. But in one vision, the hospitals remain at the center of health data, upholding standards and overseeing much of its flow. In the opposing view, all of us have access to our data, in whatever standard, and are able to manage and share it through a secure and vibrant network. I'll let you guess which side I'm on.

First, a bit of background. Epic is perhaps the greatest entrepreneurial success story in health care technology. Headquartered on a meticulously designed campus outside of Madison, Wisconsin, it produces big and expensive enterprise software programs for hospitals. This software links the various branches of a hospital, from patients' records and diagnostics to the pharmacy, the operating room, and outpatient treatment—and, of course, billing. If you look at a single Epic customer, whether Cleveland Clinic or Kaiser Permanente, the promise of electronic medical records comes to life. You can track the journey of a patient through the corridors, from one department to the next. You can see the tests, the prescriptions, the doctors' notes. You can see practically everything until the patient steps out of the hospital. At that point, though, the Epic screen, for all intents and purposes, goes blank.

You might think that a system that loses track of customers like that is flawed. But Epic's customers are the hospitals. And these systems fit their needs. If one hospital has records on a certain patient, it makes it much harder for a doctor to send that patient to a competing hospital. What's more, if the hospital can link pharmacies and nursing homes and rehab centers to its single copy of Epic, all of the patients receive coordinated care in a closed system. It gives the hospital control and something close to monopoly pricing. After all, unhappy patients are less likely to leave if their medical records stay behind. A single system like Epic is a hospital's dream.

It's the inverse of athenahealth. A doctor using our system can manage patients as they move through the ecosystem of health care, overseeing medications, lab reports, checkups, and, yes, billing. Practically everyone's data works on our Web application, athenaNet. Openness is at the heart of our business model. However, when that patient enters a hospital running on Epic, the data flow, traditionally, has come to a halt.

Every technology company's goal in our nook of the industry, naturally, is to build systems that follow a patient's medical care. Epic is a titan inside hospitals, with installations in three hundred of the five hundred biggest in the country. Our strength has traditionally been outside the hospitals. One logical solution would be to open our systems to each other. That was our hope. Another option was to use the leverage at hand to tame and co-opt the competition. That appeared to be what some of the hospitals were using Epic to do, and when we saw this strategy start to play out, we were alarmed.

Like any company, we face mortal threats. There is always the possibility that some other company will come along and outperform or outmaneuver us, and we will be eaten or fade from the scene. It's a common story in technology. Think of Netscape, Compaq, and, more recently, Nokia and BlackBerry. It's also true that companies use technology to lock down markets and force competitors to their knees, or their graves.

That is what this story is about. It involves regional powerhouses working with Epic to extend their dominance over local health economics. It is an effort to sustain the status quo—the health care industry that revolves around a group of big hospitals. We shouldn't be surprised that hospital executives focus on saving their own institutions. That's their job. But at times their strategy hinges on withholding information: medical records not getting to competing doctors, patients not learning about better deals down the road. And the strategy works to keep potential competitors—which are precisely what the industry needs—in the dark.

This is an example of how it works. In New Haven, the Yale University

Medical Center is the regional behemoth. If you live in southern Connecticut and are diagnosed with an aggressive cancer or need a liver transplant, you want it done at Yale. This is Yale's leverage. Now Yale, like other big medical centers, just became an Epic customer. It recently spent more than $250 million to buy and install the system. This is a massive undertaking. It involves brigades of technicians and consultants, who reroute and recode every bit of information traveling through the hospital's network.

Outside the hospital are hundreds of doctors and medical practices. They have their own information systems, which lay claim to many of the same patients. What's more, they can increasingly use technology to sniff out the best deals for their patients and steer them away from the expensive hospital. As medical practices take more patients on risk contracts, overseeing each patient's health for a fixed sum, finding such deals will feed their bottom line. It will be central to their business. As you can imagine, any trend in which doctors find the best deals for their patients is extremely threatening to the highest cost provider, which is usually the biggest hospital. Shopping puts its entire business model at risk, because those overpriced colonoscopies and CT scans underwrite massive building projects, not to mention fat executive salaries and loads of inefficiency.

I often think of these big research hospitals as duchies somewhere in middle Europe. The duke is interdependent with the villagers and peasants, but he views them as his servants. They regard him as an authority in a higher order, occupying a place between themselves and God. For as long as anyone can remember, they have tended his vineyards, milked his cows, plowed his fields, and harvested his wheat. They're blissfully ignorant and they work for him. But then a problem emerges. Some upstart in Mainz has built a printing press, and leaflets are coming into the duchy, where some of the villagers have learned to read. Now they're making noises about selling some of their crops in other markets, where they can fetch better prices. It's a revolution!

The duke is beside himself with worry. His nervous finger wears a hole through his ermine cloak. They're breaking away. He's losing control. He's not only worried about himself, but also the town. Some might say that he exploits the villagers, but he uses the profits to build the clock tower and dig the well. In his mind, he *is* the town. What can he do? He's not a cruel man, and he resists the suggestion to arrest the ringleaders and flay them. Instead he issues an ultimatum in his own leaflet. From this day forward, anyone who conducts business outside his system will be barred from the duchy. No wine from the vineyard, no water from the well, no protection from the troops. Excommunication from the church. Take that, you scurvy ingrates.

In recent years, duchies like Yale have won the allegiance of the villagers or doctors the old-fashioned way: They've bought them. In an acquiring frenzy, they've laid claim to thousands of patients by purchasing practices and turning doctors into employees. But that's very expensive. It's more economical to turn the equation around, and control the doctors without buying them. You keep them off the payroll, which saves a bundle, and then simply threaten to bar their access to the hospital if they don't play nice.

The leverage for this is information. A few years back, Yale sent messages to doctors in the region inviting them to share an opportunity. The doctors could buy heavily subsidized licenses for Epic software, and then use them to share their patient records with the hospital. The implication for not getting on board was clear: Those practices that chose to stay outside the Epic ecosystem would lose the ability to connect and exchange information with Yale. If their patients got sick and ended up at Yale, they were unlikely to get information back to keep track of their care, and would risk losing their patients to another doctor hooked up to Yale. This was powerful leverage in southern Connecticut, where the Yale system, with its million-dollar oncologists and celebrity cardiologists, stands supreme in tertiary care.

We saw this drama taking place across the country. And in each area, many of our customers said they felt pressure to buy Epic—and to drop us. In theory, they could keep paying the subscription for our system as well, entering all the data twice, once for Epic and once on our system. They could also stroll outside and burn hundred-dollar bills. It wasn't going to happen.

I was convinced that this strategy would fail. It was based on two backward assumptions. The first was regional dominance. In markets in which people can travel and information is ubiquitous, such a regional play is doomed. It is true that most of us don't have the resources of a Steve Jobs, who could fly to Memphis for his transplant. But increasingly, we will have access to information about the best bargains and highest performers, and we will travel to them. What's more, a hospital's ecosystem now includes national players. The retail chain Target, for example, runs clinics around the country. When the big hospitals in Minneapolis pushed it toward Epic, Target pushed back. Why would a national chain ever want to link into fifty or one hundred closed biospheres around the country? It's clear to me that the regional play is based on the past, not the future.

The second questionable assumption is that hospitals could use a single closed system to lock down an industry. As far as I see it, patients increasingly are going to be producing, consuming, and demanding access to their own medical data. They're going to want to call it up on their smart phones and tablets. And they won't just look at this data. They'll also have tools to create mash-ups with it, blending it with their jogging routines, diets, vitamins, sleep patterns. Health data is going to be part of our lives, and we are not going to settle for a single system imposed by big hospitals or a Wisconsin-based software company, or, for that matter, athenahealth or anyone else.

While I'm convinced that openness will ultimately prevail over opacity, I also recognize that this vision might not come into sparkling focus for a few years, maybe even a decade. And so during those crucial months of 2013, I worried that, unless we resolved this issue with Epic and the hospitals, Epic's faulty assumptions might be strong enough over the next several years to scare away thousands of our clients and pummel our business. In short, we could be both right and hurting. Those two conditions are not mutually exclusive.

Epic, after all, is a powerful company, and in many respects a great one. It was started in the midseventies when Judy Faulkner, a computer science graduate student at the University of Wisconsin, wrote a program to track and centralize patient information. She used a programming language called MUMPS (Massachusetts General Hospital Utility Multi-Programming System). Nearly forty years later, Epic systems dominate U.S. hospitals and hold the electronic records of some 135 million patients.

The company recruits heavily from Faulkner's alma mater, and it teaches its recruits how to program in the venerable MUMPS language. (That tends to lock down talent, because job hunting with MUMPS expertise in the rest of the tech world is like leaning on Latin to swing a job in a parish church.) Faulkner, who still runs the privately held company, is a billionaire, according to *Forbes*. She's extremely private and stays out of the press.

The company occupies a large chunk of farmland in Verona, Wisconsin, just outside Madison. Its "Intergalactic Headquarters" looks like a giant horseshoe in the fields. Everything about it, I've been told, is designed to express beauty, perfection, even sustainability. It is powered by on-site solar and geothermal plants. The modules each have a theme, from Africa and Andromeda to a Wild West complete with stagecoaches. There are tunnels that pass through hell, complete with underworld images. To climb up their celestial work space, developers mount a Stairway to Heaven. The workmanship is exquisite. Not a single nail head is exposed. Expenses do not appear to be the chief concern.

Through the years, I've been told, a list of "commandments" has circulated among the Epic workforce. Two of them: Never go public and never make a deal. Those two commandments share a common theme: maintaining control. Going public would bring in a bunch of investors who would have a big say in the company's direction (and might object to some of the spending in the Intergalactic Headquarters). Essentially, it's a loss of control in exchange for capital. Epic doesn't need it or want it. Fair enough. The commandment against deals is similar. By their very nature, deals dilute Epic's formula, either driving down prices or introducing interlopers into their carefully honed software product.

In a word, Epic wants to go it alone in a world it can define and control. This safeguards the quality of its product and services. Needless to say, it makes it difficult to negotiate with the company. But when Epic's customers have their boot placed firmly in the vicinity of our corporate windpipe, what else can we do?

Epic's marketing strategy is little short of genius. Much like a luxury country club, it informs select hospitals that they qualify for its product. Since its client roster is a who's who of name-brand hospitals, admission to the Epic club seems tantamount to making the weekend cut at the Masters. Like an exclusive club, of course, it costs big bucks, and comes with an extensive list of bylaws. For example, prospective clients, once approved, must buy all modules of the Epic system, in many cases, about thirty of them. They must also send a group of chosen "super-users" to the Wisconsin campus every year. They must set up the modules as Epic dictates, and sign a legal contract promising never to disparage the company.

The system also requires years to install. In my neighborhood, Partners is spending $1 billion on an Epic installation that will take nearly three years to fully implement. That comes to about $1 million a day (or three hundred overpriced colonoscopies). The whole place is crawling with consultants. (Not to advertise in these pages, but our subscription model would cost a fraction as much; the installation and consulting budget would be negligible by comparison.)

In return for the Epic investment, hospitals receive the industry standard. It's considered reliable, and does a solid job on coding and billing, the heart of a hospital's revenue stream. In recent years, Epic has become the consensus option for big spenders, much the way IBM was a half century ago. It's long been said that you can't get fired for buying the industry standard. But you can certainly miss important trends—like the Internet.

Epic, after all, is a product that dates back to the 1970s, when the definition of a supermodern hospital was one that stored its data on a big honking computer flipping through punch cards. This machine, running software written in MUMPS, was the brains of the system. It was not connected to anything outside the hospital. Why would it be?

For a decade or two, this didn't seem to bother Epic's customers. Sure, the rest of the corporate world was racing to link up with customers and suppliers online. Whether they were selling soap or soda pop, their business depended on seamless communications. Epic, by contrast, was selling to an industry operating in a bubble. None of the usual metrics applied. In health care, high cost = profits. Savings = lost revenue. Customers = . . . Well, now that you mention it, who exactly were their customers? And why should they share any information with them? In this alternate universe, it is still possible for hospital administrators to cling to the idea that they can build their own closed fiefdoms, that they can strong-arm doctors into joining them, that the $2.7 trillion health care economy can revolve around hospitals and run on MUMPS.

We pushed Epic to let us build bridges into their system, but could not reach an agreement. They made noises about security issues, potential interruptions to "seamless" flows of data. But as I see it, it just didn't fit their business plan. They seemed to be intent on building stand-alone biospheres.

We fought back. First we whined to Dr. Farzad Mostashari, the national coordinator for health IT under President Obama (until late 2013). Mostashari was a central architect of the 2009 stimulus bill that offered billions in rewards for doctors who invested in electronic health records. He was appalled to see how EHRs were being used to fortify hospital monopolies. He understood that more than 90 percent of health care occurs outside of hospitals. And while I may criticize the government's heavy hand in the industry, and while Mostashari and I differ on the economics of a data marketplace, he and his team saw electronic data as a catalyst for change.

The vision behind the EHR stimulus, after all, is to create a modern data economy, one in which everyone in the industry will be able to participate. This means following more than three hundred million individuals, and accessing (through secure channels and with the patients' permission) the relevant data from the records wherever these people go. No more clipboards. No more phone calls to get past prescription records. And much more data is available for the patient, wherever and whenever he or she wants it, at the doctor's office, on the smart phone, at the scene of an accident. For this, systems must be able to talk to each other and exchange data. More than that, it requires a market, where hospitals, clinics, labs, and private practices can charge each other fees for data, creating a sustainable market for it. This vast universe of data will never be cloistered on a single system. Instead, all systems should be able to trade data, just the way modern industries do on the Internet. The government regulators agreed with much of this, but they could not forbid hospitals from pursuing their Epic-based strategy.

So the team in our Epic war room moved to the referral game. This involved collecting groups of our own clients who were never going to sell out to their local hospitals, but controlled large numbers of referrals that those hospitals coveted. Then our war room team took these clients, such as the New Haven Independent Physician Association, to a number of hospitals. They stressed the importance of seamless connections for referrals and made it clear that they would be much more likely to send their patients to hospitals they could connect with. If Epic could build a bridge to athenaNet, fine. If not, more accommodating hospitals would likely gain more of their business. The size of these groups made this message meaningful. At this point, Epic started to hear from its own hospital clients that maybe they should open up the system a tad.

This was a positive development, but we couldn't wait for Epic to build bridges from its system. Our future was at stake. So we looked for a way to worm our way inside these hospital biospheres. We needed something like a Trojan horse. Luckily, we had the perfect vehicle. Early in 2013, we had paid nearly $400 million for Epocrates, a Silicon Valley company that offers the number one most popular mobile application for doctors. More than 330,000 health care professionals throughout the country regularly consult the Epocrates app on their smart phones for clinical information, especially about medicines and side effects. This is our beachhead in doctors' pockets.

Here's how we plan to worm our way in. Each doctor on Epocrates will get free access on their phones or tablets to "network face sheets." Without logging in to any system at all, they'll see a consolidated view of any patient they're treating. If the hospital they admit to has its data locked up on a closed system, they will have the option of sending an electronic message, saying, in effect: Get connected.

Not all of the data on these face sheets will come from athenaNet, and that's a crucial point. We do not control a biosphere. To populate these pages with all of the relevant data, we'll need to work with other companies. This way, we'll take on a closed system with an open one.

In the summer of 2013, a few weeks after coming up with our face sheet strategy, one of our team got a message from a colleague at Epic. It suggested that we work together on building some sort of bridge between the systems. So now the discussion has progressed. It started with "we can't," progressed to "we won't," and is finally at, "we will, a little." The first breakthrough came in October, when New York's Memorial Sloan Kettering, one of the giants in cancer therapy and research, agreed to pioneer a connection out of Epic onto our network. Others no doubt will follow.

But Epic is still using its hospital leverage to defend its biosphere. It does this by charging the hospitals—its customers—a small fee for every data transfer with a non-Epic entity. Let's say a doctor who's not on Epic refers her patient to Sloan Kettering. The hospital must pay a dollar or two for that patient's records. This is like a tax for going outside of the biosphere. Hospitals won't have to pay it if they can convert these doctors into Epic customers. It represents a switch in tactics, from commandments to a tax, but it continues to support the biosphere with the hospital at the center of health information.

No matter. Epic's journey from "impossible" through "no" to "yes, but you have to pay me" has been remarkably quick. I'm glad (and relieved) that Judy Faulkner and I are talking price.

Our two strategies, of course, could not be more different, nor could our vision of the future of health care. Epic believes in closed systems that can be engineered, controlled, perfected. Their Intergalactic Headquarters embodies this philosophy. The whole world—indeed, the entire universe—fits into the Wisconsin campus, all of it designed in loving, meticulous, and expensive detail. This is a vision hospitals can relate to. You might call it intelligent design. And if you see Epic humming along inside one of its hospitals, it's a beautiful thing.

We, by contrast, love a good mess. We prefer the chaos of a marketplace, a Darwinian struggle in which entrepreneurs develop a potpourri of products and services. Many of them will start out primitive. Most will fail. But if a few of these entrepreneurs solve even simple customer problems, they can earn their way into the exam rooms or back offices of practices and hospitals. In fact, our goal is to nurture these disrupters and turn them into partners.

CHAPTER TEN

More Disruption, Please

On a brilliant October morning on the coast of Maine, I pulled on a loincloth and a ragged, sleeveless T-shirt riddled with holes. I attached a bushy beard to my face, grabbed a pike, and ran to the front of a crowd of startled health care entrepreneurs. This was our third annual More Disruption, Please gathering, and I was dressed like a caveman to make a simple point: Primitive apps are OK. In fact, they can change the world.

The entrepreneurs in the audience probably didn't find this message flattering. But I'm convinced that in health care technology, primitive is where the opportunities lie, and that simple, affordable systems will give birth to the disruption we're aching for. I didn't speak too much in my rustic getup. Instead I introduced one of my favorite professors from Harvard Business School, Clayton Christensen, who drove home the point much more eloquently than I did with my pike and loincloth.

Clay towered before the gathering, all six foot eight of him. A few years ago, he told us, he had suffered a stroke. It affected the part of his brain that governed speech. So he had to relearn English. He spoke to us a bit more slowly than he used to, choosing his words with care. But this deliberate style made his message resonate even more powerfully.

Think of a company that sells advanced technology to big hospitals, he said. Its managers have been taught since their school days to focus relentlessly on their best customers. That's the business school mantra. And what do those customers need? Well, they already have last year's model. So the key is to figure out what other features they would value, and to sell them an updated version. Naturally, it will be more expensive.

Most tech companies follow this path. In health care's upper right quadrant, where price often is no object, they deliver scandalously expensive technology, from imaging to data storage and proton beam accelerators. Selling in markets where price is no object is great business. But there's one challenge: Technology development usually outpaces the ability of humans to adapt to it. So the incumbent tech companies are soon selling systems that are more advanced, and with more features, than their customers can handle. Almost all of their customers, as you might expect, are rich.

Below them lies the vast middle class of health care. That's the market for disruptive technology. Loads of companies and small practices in the industry have tech budgets that run in the thousands or tens of thousands of dollars—not millions or hundreds of millions. The trick is to help them solve their problems with something they can afford. It doesn't have to be perfect. It doesn't even have to be particularly good. It can evolve later. The key is to establish a foothold in the market now. For that, it has to outperform a clipboard hitched to a pen with tape wrapped around it, an overworked fax machine, or a nurse taking information from a computer and writing into a ledger, or vice versa. In this world, many primitive Internet technologies represent the future. A huge underserved market is hungrily awaiting them.

We want to help these entrepreneurs reach them. It's part of our core strategy. The premise is that health care desperately needs brilliant people coming up with breakthrough ideas. The more, the better.

Most of those people—the vast majority—aren't employed by athena-health or any other single company. As Bill Joy, the co-founder of Sun Microsystems, has famously declared, "No matter who you are, most of the smartest people work for someone else." Yet even though these people don't work for us, they can work with us, reaching customers on our network. This is the idea behind More Disruption, Please, or MDP. It will feed into our own health data app store, following the models of Apple and Google and the enterprise software powerhouse, Salesforce .com. It is the antithesis of a closed and uniform ecosystem, like Epic's.

More than a single company, we're intent on creating a vast platform for health data. Everything on this platform must meet our security and patient privacy standards, be sold as a service (with only implementation fees up front), and measure the outcomes it promises. Within those constraints, we'll welcome any idea, no matter how crazy, as long as it meets at least one of three conditions: It must drive revenue to our customers, take work off their plate, or improve their results. If an app is successful, our service grows richer, the entrepreneur makes money—and we keep a slice of the revenue. Win-win-win.

These entrepreneurs, I should add, have chosen a rough road. Plenty of tech visionaries, from AOL's Steve Case to the leaders of Google, have attempted to colonize the hostile health care information economy, and have retreated, battered and bruised. Even when selling to enterprises, there are few buyers in health care, and their purchasing decisions often appear to defy reason. Ideas have to percolate through layers of bureaucracy. There are meetings, and lots of questions. Can it be incorporated into our legacy IT system? What are the risks? Let's consult and have another meeting. Next month, perhaps? The system conspires against newcomers.

This is especially true if the newcomers threaten a comfy status quo—which is almost always the case. Remember Gladys, our prototypical claims administrator at a medical group? She has devoted a career to mastering a set of arcane details. Complexity is her friend. It protects her livelihood. And with this new program any idiot could do the same job! Or worse, the machine might handle it alone, assuming the program works, which of course it won't. . . .

Entrenched ranks in every industry resist innovation. But in health care, the opposition is especially fierce. This happens for two reasons. First, much of the industry is impervious to cost constraints. If you talk about lowering costs at a big research hospital, executives yawn. The second reason is that the medical industry is in the business of saving lives. That one fact comes in handy not only to justify limitless expense and inefficiency but also to resist change. The Hippocratic oath is a big deal in health care, and a new procedure could kill people. Medical errors, of course, kill people too—by some estimates, two hundred thousand per year. So new efficiencies could also save lives. In fact, they do. But in a profession whose founding commandment is *primum non nocere,* or "first, do no harm," there's always a convenient excuse for saying no.

This beats down entrepreneurs. And investors stay clear of the industry. As a result the digital start-up scene is a moonscape. In 2012, a mere $1.4 billion of venture funding trickled into digital health start-ups. That's a tiny number for a $2.7 trillion industry, and it's one reason we felt we needed to start MDP. If start-ups get their technologies onto our network, they can reach a fast-growing customer base of fifty thousand–plus providers. So while the entrepreneurs at our gathering appreciate the beauty of our coastal campus in Maine, enjoy the sailing, the lobster dinner, and the bowling, the greatest appeal is to get onto our network and reach customers.

This is far from charity on our part. If we go it alone in providing cloud-based services, the benefits of the technology will plummet. In that case, most information about health care will remain on other networks, from closed hospital biospheres to groups on Facebook and word-of-mouth connections. But if a true marketplace develops in the cloud, if customers have multiple choices for nearly every product and service, if they can search and compare them, and share notes about them on the same platform, then the industry will grow like crazy. This will change the economics for the entire industry and drive explosive growth in cloud companies—including, we hope, our own.

Between sessions at the conference, I scan the list of entrepreneurs and their technologies. For anyone who has surfed a smart phone app store, this stuff looks pretty basic. I'd almost say boring. Visitors from other industries, such as e-commerce or logistics, might view these technologies as throwbacks from the late 1990s, when companies were just starting to adapt to the Internet. This, of course, is what health care is embarking upon right now. So naturally the radical and disruptive stuff, as a certain caveman would say, is primitive.

One start-up, Beyond Lucid, provides communications for emergency response teams. Say an ambulance unit gets a call for a woman who has collapsed in her apartment. They can perform tests on-site, taking her pulse and blood pressure, and send this data along with the patient's electronic health record to the emergency room so that the right team and technologies will be deployed there and ready to receive her. You might think that hospitals equipped with gamma knives and telemanipulators would have such links in place. Not so.

The status quo in many emergency response teams is eerily similar to our New Orleans ambulances in the early nineties. It's a walkie-talkie barking to some hospital resident, who then has to relay the information—more barking—to everyone within earshot. I have ridden with dozens of ambulance crews in many urban and rural markets. Many have electronic medical records on board. But none of them is used for care, or to provide advance information about the patient to the hospital. For these mission-critical tasks, the primary tools were the Sharpie pen on three-inch tape and the walkie-talkie. In some cases, says Jonathon Feit, Beyond Lucid's CEO, the medic will administer tests on-site, write the results with a Sharpie on the back of his hand, and later read them to doctors when bringing in the patient. With a status quo like that, a basic communications link can bring dramatic improvement.

Or consider CareSync. Amy Gleason, a mother in the Tampa area, co-founded this company after her daughter, Morgan, was diagnosed with juvenile dermatomyositis, a complex autoimmune disease that requires loads of treatment and medication. As they waded into the hospital world, they soon encountered serious information glitches. First, many of Morgan's medical records were incomplete or wrong. Other times, they were packed in voluminous binders that doctors had no time or patience to read. Vital information was inaccessible.

This represented a market opportunity. Now Amy is the chief operating officer of CareSync. The company employs people to track down the far-flung information about customers' tests, diagnoses, and medications, and to summarize them in a form that doctors can digest.

In terms of technology, CareSync is closer to fourteenth-century Benedictine monks than to Facebook or Google. The work is carried out by human beings who track down information and compile it. Primitive, yes, but this service is filling a black hole in the health care market. And here's the important point: While it might start in a very basic form, it doesn't have to stay that way. It can evolve. That is what's wonderful—and disruptive—about primitive technologies.

While CareSync focuses on a small niche, another start-up, RegisterPatient.com, reaches out to everyone who has ever called up for an appointment and been put on hold. Its software allows people to sign up for appointments online, fill out e-registration forms, receive care alerts, manage referrals, and request prescriptions. It's about what you'd expect if Amazon.com got into the medicine business, which is precisely the point. In fact, it's Amazon from about ten years ago. This type of service can and will grow more sophisticated, and continue to shake up the industry (in a good way).

The theme of tech evolution reminds me of the transistor radio. When I was a kid, in the seventies, our parents had great big stereos in the living room. Many of them produced fabulous sound. They also cost more than $1,000 and were impossible to move. Assume that a kid back then could earn $4 an hour doing odd jobs. A good stereo cost 250 hours of work, and each record album cost another hour. Kids, clearly, weren't the target market. Instead, many of us would drop about $20 on a transistor radio. The sound quality was dreadful, often similar to a kazoo. But the radios were cheap and we could carry them around.

Cash-poor kids were the untapped market. The established hi-fi companies like Marantz and Zenith were racing up the quality curve and selling to audiophiles and deep-pocketed wannabes. For these companies, it was as if we didn't exist. Sometime in the future, when we got real jobs and living rooms with grown-up furniture, maybe we could graduate to their products.

While the early transistor radios were primitive, they evolved. First, they got big. In the late seventies, people walked around the city carrying huge radios, so-called boom boxes, on their shoulders. The sound, while intrusive, was much improved. Then, in 1979, Sony launched the Walkman. The quality still wasn't up there with the living room stereos, but it was getting closer. And with cassette tapes, we didn't need to buy as many albums anymore. We could copy them from our friends. For the music industry, this was disruptive.

A huge market evolved for mobile music. Apple's iPod, introduced in 2001, allowed people to carry entire record collections in their pockets, and listen to sound that was fine (for all but the vinyl snobs). Now mobile music not only dwarfs the traditional stereo business, it has also changed the way we experience music. The same revolution has convulsed the industries that used to make cameras, typewriters, fax machines, and telephones. All of these devices now reside in one machine, the smart phone.

So why can't Amy Gleason and her daughter and the doctors caring for her access all the medical information they want and need from that device? Soon they will, I predict. It won't begin with a magical suite of integrated applications, but instead with one basic and useful app. And then another, and another. Perhaps one will be CareSync. Many of them, I'm hoping, will be available on our platform and work with every kind of device. Doctors will access some of them on the Epocrates app. Perhaps consumers will, too. Early on, hospital executives will pooh-pooh these innovations, dismissing them as primitive. But they will eventually turn the industry upside down. I'll be applauding wildly from a front-row seat.

At one point in his talk, Clay showed us a slide of the layout of an old tooling mill in Pontiac, Michigan. It had about sixteen different machine sectors, each one with a specific job. One stretched a piece of metal, another pressed it, a third added gearing, buffered, or annealed it. This tooling mill was flexible. It could take a metal cylinder and turn it into practically anything. This flexibility, while convenient for industrial customers, made for daunting complexity and sky-high costs, because each variable introduced new questions about how to manage and schedule it. Each job was unique. This was the opposite of a focused factory, which optimizes around a single and predictable job.

In this way, he said, the tooling mill resembles a hospital. It too is set up to handle any job, and it comes up with a different schedule and route for each patient. This is highly inefficient, of course, and unpredictable, as million-dollar surgeons and ten-million-dollar machines often wait around for work. As my kids might say, it's random.

Some of this randomness is inevitable because hospitals, unlike auto plants, need to be able to handle a wide range of emergencies. But they also do a lot of standard and predictable work. What pressure do they face to carry out those jobs more efficiently and to cut costs? I think this disruption has to come from outside—and a good dose of it from fellow MDP members.

But this doesn't mean the entrepreneurs should start with hospitals. Sure, a lot of them might look at the inefficiencies in hospitals and see opportunities. No doubt there are jobs, maybe pharmacy or inventory management, that they could handle much better. All that's needed, they might think, is a thirty-minute session to demo the technology for a hospital administrator or two. And then, just imagine the upside. If entrepreneurs can sell their apps to Partners, or to Mayo, they'll have a breakthrough contract, legitimacy, a brand. They'll be in the big time.

Clay told them not to bother, and I agree. His argument is that an entrepreneur who attempts to sell to a big enterprise inevitably has to tweak the product again and again to satisfy various needs and interest groups inside the hospital. The process it goes through strips out the innovations that threaten the status quo. It becomes an extension of the legacy system, and is bound to it. In this way, the prospect of a big contract leads the entrepreneur down the wrong road.

Furthermore, trying to get big companies to buy an improved version of something they already have is a waste of time. Let's say a hospital has a mediocre scheduling program. It's slow. It doesn't sync to the calendar. Its interface is ugly and confusing. You and your friends would never put up with it. But the hospital has probably bought that software from a supplier it knows. The relationship has gone on for years. These people, customer and supplier, go on golf outings. They might eat together once or twice a year at a fabulous restaurant. Sure, people bellyache about the technology, but people always bellyache. Why would the hospital switch something that works, albeit badly, for your app, which might not work at all? What's more, often an app from a major supplier is guaranteed to work with everything else the hospital has in place. Why would the hospital risk that to try out a sexier app from an untested upstart? Not going to happen!

I see this in my own company. We have lame coffee machines. Lots of people here, including me, experience great coffee at home and in coffee shops. Yet at work, the coffee is tasteless. The milk is powdered. Just like hospitals, it seems, we stick with a known bad over a possible good.

I looked into this for this book, and I learned that using milk represents a danger (unless you have a super self-cleaning machine). It can rot. The vendor who provides these machines deals with plumbing, connecting the water supply through filters. The same vendor also cleans the filters and replenishes the tasteless beans on a regular basis. So when viewed through the eyes of the facilities team, what I interpreted as lousy coffee is instead a safe and hygienic service provided by a reliable company at a decent price. What surprised me the most was that they had never received a complaint about the coffee until I nosed around. In any case, we have a coffee solution, and it will be hard to change.

This inertia is hard to overcome. So in every corporate market from coffee machines to Post-it notes, the fabulous market opportunity is not in replacing bad with better. The trick instead is to provide something the customers simply don't have. That means coming up with affordable apps or services that have long been beyond the range of smaller medical practices. It might be a job they currently do by hand, or perhaps one they pay the hospital to do. Some of the best markets are in the jobs they hate and suck at.

That's the market we sold to in our early days at athenahealth. More sophisticated billing and patient management programs were out there. But a vast group of smaller practices and clinics could never afford them. And if they could scrape together the money, they could not afford the staff to use them properly. So we showed up with the market's first cloud-based business service. It wasn't such an amazing service at first. But it was free to implement. And athenaNet would harness it to deal with all the paperwork they absolutely hated. All we asked for in return was a share of the collections we brought in. In their eyes, we replaced nothing with something that worked. In this sense, athenaNet was like the transistor radio. It was primitive, but accessible. Customers didn't have to buy anything. They just paid for subscriptions, and if they didn't like it, they stopped paying. This was a low barrier to entry. Most important, the service could (and did) evolve.

And it's not just the service that evolves. An entire industry does. If you arm the small-fry and the newcomers with affordable tools, the technology evolves faster than people ask it to, until eventually they can use it to compete with the giants, and even topple them. The tools are essential. I know from experience, because we lacked them in the nineties. So even though we had great dreams of reinventing childbirth in America, we wasted our time on fools' errands. We literally had someone drive around and look in the books at hospitals and clinics to count the babies of ours that were delivered. We were blind. But now—without blowing our horn excessively—that service is available. Startups like Florida Woman Care have access to the information they need. They're using it to attack the very same market we went after. They are wresting market share from big hospitals—and making money.

In 1998, when Clay Christensen carried out his study on the convoluted manufacturing plant, U.S. manufacturers were under intense competitive pressure, mostly from the Japanese. They had to raise efficiency and reduce costs, or they were dead. It shows just how backward health care is that a twenty-five-year-old example from an old-line industry is still relevant. In fact, some hospital executives still believe that they can avoid the competitive pressures that rained down on manufacturing all those years ago. After all, health care is different. People die.

Still, the real world is closing in. Competition is rising. Consumers, corporations, and the economy cannot bankroll the status quo for much longer, and hospitals' biggest revenue source, inpatient treatment, is in decline. Nights in the hospital are falling for every age group. So it might make sense to take a look at how manufacturing tackled its competitive issues—and what opportunities a similar process might open up in health care.

In the eighties and nineties, consultants flew from one troubled manufacturer to the next and delivered a sobering message. They couldn't do everything. They had to figure out what they were best at—their core competency—and focus on that. It was far better to excel in one area than to muddle along in a dozen. (It's interesting that consultants themselves are now subject to very similar forces. The cloud commoditizes their knowledge and insights, and they have to dig deep to find their own core competency.)

How could companies figure out what they were best at? How could they detect the waste and sloppiness in their operations? For this, they had to start measuring their operations. Only when they had numbers could they begin to manage their businesses scientifically. This was called reengineering. It often involved implementing big enterprise software programs, such as Oracle or Germany's SAP. (That way, managers could blame painful decisions on the software. "Jeez, I'd sure like to keep this twenty-year-old assembly line running, but there doesn't seem to be a label for it on this software program.") Once implemented, the software started churning out numbers and measurements of performance. Managers for the first time could see each unit's cost, capacity utilization, error rate, customer satisfaction, and profitability. Suddenly, it wasn't so hard to figure out what they were good at—and what they stank at. It was clear as day.

This analysis took what seemed like long, integrated operations and broke them into dozens or hundreds of measurable pieces. Then the companies began hiring outside specialists to handle the jobs they stank at. They got rid of their cafeteria staff (they weren't a restaurant company!) and hired a food service. Many of them dumped human resources. They started to ship low-margin assembly work to specialized plants in Mexico or China. This process was no party. It devastated towns throughout America's Rust Belt. But the alternative was even grimmer.

At this point in my story, I can already hear the hospital execs starting to grumble. "We don't run a manufacturing plant!" they're saying. "We cannot cut up our work, much less our patients, and ship them every which way. We're different."

This is true. Here in Boston, we got a vivid and inspiring view of just how different hospitals are, and how their often maddeningly helter-skelter operations can adapt to emergencies. On April 15, 2013, terrorist bombs at the Boston Marathon killed three people instantly and left a staggering 263 with injuries, many of them grievous. Over the following hours, hospitals in the area carried out lifesaving surgery on scores of patients. They amputated limbs and patched up wounds. They dealt with concussions and shock, and amid mayhem they created order. From one hour to the next, they designed 263 patient treatments, many of them unique. And not a single wounded patient died. On that tragic day, the doctors, nurses, medics, ambulance drivers, and techs of Boston area hospitals batted a thousand.

It's greatness like this, and heroism, that brings tears to our eyes and can lead us to give hospitals a break. But we cannot afford to. For our health and our economy, they must figure out how to organize and optimize the planned part of their business, which is most of it, while leaving adequate flexibility for emergencies.

Others argue that medicine deserves a break from traditional metrics because the core of the business, the intense person-to-person relationship between the doctor and the patient, is unique. It resists measurement and, in the best of cases, should be heedless of time. The focus should be to maximize and deepen these encounters. If they're inefficient, that's OK.

I agree. But here's the point, which may seem counterintuitive: The best way to support and facilitate the special person-to-person contact is to run the rest of the operation with the efficiency of an Amazon fulfillment warehouse.

The first goal should be to reduce idle capacity. High-paid people often hang around killing time in health care because, as I've said, the whole process is random. Some of it always will be. But if a certain job requires analysis or expertise, hospitals and medical practices may be able to outsource it to a specialist on the Internet. Creating pods of such experts is a promising market for entrepreneurs.

One example is Radisphere, a Cleveland-based start-up (on whose board I sit). The company's cloud-based service provides expert analysis of the medical images that the health care industry churns outs in dizzying quantity. Medical imaging accounts for 7.5 percent of the health care spend, or $200 billion. (Just for context, that is roughly equivalent to the gross domestic product of Ireland.) Images are the gatekeepers for medical care. A doctor rarely even scratches the skin with a scalpel without a close look at what's underneath it, preferably from a number of different angles. For this reason, imaging is growing at an astounding 14 percent (which puts it on track to reach Israel's GDP within a year or two). Reducing this runaway spending, of course, is important for the economy. Equally important is to speed up and improve the analysis. That's vital for our health.

The trouble for many hospitals is that medical images are proliferating faster than they can analyze them. So they expand their radiology teams. But it's very hard to calibrate how many radiologists to staff, and what types of expertise they should have. The traffic of images fluctuates, which means that radiologists are either swamped or bored. This hurts the bottom line and, more importantly, patient care.

Let's say a doctor orders up a CT scan before a patient goes into liver surgery. The team needs that image, along with the analysis of what it shows, before commencing the surgery. But if there's a backlog in the imaging department, the overworked radiologists might take an hour or two, or even longer, to get to it. (What's more, the liver specialist might be off duty, and the one who ends up with these images might be better at brains or breasts.) If a one-hour surgery takes five hours because you're waiting four hours for an image, you're paying five times as much for the team, the bed, the slot in the operating room. Meanwhile, in some cases, the patient's condition worsens.

Manufacturers provide a lesson here. In the 1980s, many American plant managers adopted a Japanese process called Just In Time production. It called for a finely tuned network of suppliers to deliver all of the components just as they were needed. No more digging around through warehouses for inventory, or ordering components that would take a day or a week to deliver. The necessary parts arrived every few minutes. This eliminated enormous waste and it distributed responsibility to a host of partners. Suppliers were all too aware that an entire manufacturing operation hinged upon their success in delivering parts on time. Their own livelihood was also at stake. If they missed deadlines, they lost the contract. Their business, in short, was to be on time.

That's what Radisphere offers. With its team of more than 150 radiologists, it delivers results within established deadlines. Possible strokes need images processed and analyzed within twenty minutes. Less urgent reports, perhaps for a scheduled knee-replacement surgery, might take a day.

Just as important as the timing is the accuracy. With a large team of radiologists, a company like Radisphere can send work to specialists in everything from kidneys to elbows. These experts get more practice than harried generalists, and quality improves. What's more, since the company's entire business is based on the quality of its radiology, it tests its experts, getting others to duplicate their work and then comparing the results, including turnaround time and accuracy. The business, like so many in the age of data, is also a laboratory.

So as this cloud business grows, what happens to the radiologists at the hospital? Do they get fired and go work at a focused factory, like Radisphere? Some of them might. But not all of the work can be outsourced. There will still be a need for radiologists on-site, who consult with doctors as part of the team. But if a hospital finds itself during slack times with an excess of in-house capacity in its radiology unit, it can rent this brainpower to Radisphere. This might mean that a radiologist at one hospital is working, a few hours a week, for the competing hospital across town, or across the country. This is the nature of the networked economy. Walls come tumbling down.

Naturally, there are risks for entrepreneurs in this business model. As I warned earlier, trying to sell hospitals an improved version of what they already have is always risky. But in a market topping $200 billion, some players just have to be hungry for savings, not to mention improved speed and quality. And once these improvements are visible, they should be hard for the rest of the industry to ignore. At least that's the hope.

Many individual start-ups will crash against the bulwarks or drown

in the moats defending the health care giants. Some, though, will succeed. As they do, more and more work and expertise will flow through
the Internet, and the once-sturdy walls protecting the status quo will
grow thinner. In some places, incumbents will vanish from the scene.
The entrepreneurs gathered in Maine, along with many others, will be
building the ecosystem to replace them. The project is immense, as are
the opportunities.

CHAPTER ELEVEN

Stark Choices

Several years ago I got a phone call from my grandmother, Cornelia. She was about ninety at this point. She had only one eye that worked and was mostly deaf, but the rest of her machinery, while no doubt failing, still had her up and around. In short, she wasn't faring too badly. "Jonny," she said. "This nice young doctor tells me I need a hysterectomy. Do you think I do?"

"No, Cornelia," I said. "You do not!"

"But," she said, "I have cancer down there."

I nearly exploded. But in the calmest voice I could muster, I asked her please to let me have a word with the doctor. Then I let him have it. If he so much as grazed my grandmother Cornelia with a scalpel, he was going to be in more trouble than he could imagine. "She doesn't need a hysterectomy," I told him. "She needs a glass of scotch."

The young gynecologist was not to be daunted. "Mr. Bush, I understand you are frustrated," he said. "But you have to understand my position. She is entitled to this care under Medicare, and I have an obligation to offer it. Your grandmother does in fact have cervical cancer."

"Doctor," I said, "would you rather die of cervical cancer after your ninety-fifth birthday or in surgery at ninety?"

"You can't know when and if surgery will kill her. I just need to give her the option, OK?"

I said OK, and that was it.

Let's just imagine for a moment that Granny had gone ahead with that operation (and survived). The average price is about $10,000. If Medicare picks up the bill for this or any other procedure that conceivably could save our lives or make us feel better, we may think, Why not? It is this calculation, with a disregard for prices, that drives health care spending to $2.7 trillion. We binge on what is covered—hoping that in the process we will get what we need or want. It can seem while we're shuffling from one exam to the next that there's no cost. But we're all paying, and plunging as a society into massive debt to do so. What's more, as I write this, we're attempting to load another twenty or thirty million people into the same dysfunctional system.

If we consumed less, we could cut these costs and live happier and healthier lives. What's more, market-based decisions on our part—shopping—would itself exert healthy pressure on runaway prices and atrocious service, and spark innovation. This pathway to rationality, however, confronts us with stark choices about what we need and what we want. And much of it boils down to our feelings about, and our acceptance of, death.

The centerpiece of the Hippocratic oath is to "do no harm." But if all medical care ends in death, how do you define "harm"? Compare these two scenarios, and tell me where the harm is. In one, a grandmother with heart failure dies in her home, surrounded by family, her pain and anxiety eased by morphine and valium administered by a trained nurse. Someone with identical symptoms dies five weeks later, alone, constrained in a hospital bed by multiple tubes. The only blessing is that she doesn't survive to see her bill.

As a society, we tend to avoid the subject of death. We'd prefer not to confront it, and the best way to do that is to postpone it. Many in the health care industry, including my grandmother's gynecologist, are all too happy to help. In surveys, 70 percent of us say we would rather die at home. And this corresponds to other studies showing that the three things people want at the end of life are absence of pain, control of their environment, and presence of family. Despite this, only three out of ten die at home. Forty percent of us do not get to die the way we would prefer. Why is this?

Part of it, no doubt, is due to fear. When the prospect of death approaches, many of us would opt to postpone it. We go to the hospital not to die, but to get better. There *must* be a drug, an answer, a cure. Maybe that $50,000 cardiac procedure will resolve the issue. Others are pushed toward the hospital by family members, eager to postpone the inevitable (and, at the same time, to keep death and dying out of the home). They're supported by a hospital industry whose values are oriented toward keeping people alive—and whose business rakes in a lot more money battling death than by holding a shaky hand and administering a morphine drip. So the hospital prevails. This is one reason that one fourth of Medicare's $586 billion annual budget is spent on medical treatment in the last year of a patient's life.

Now I don't want to waste time making policy recommendations that have zero chance of becoming law. It makes more sense to disrupt health care on the periphery, where people feel less vulnerable. If some start-up reinvents knee-replacement surgery, few would complain. But death? That's too big for policy makers. Even to mention it stirs up fear and invites attack. Remember all the fear mongering about fictitious "death panels" before Obamacare?

So why start with death? Because it's a central philosophical issue and, equally important, we do not agree on it. Some people take extraordinary measures and withstand untold discomforts to postpone death. Others elect to die at home with hospice care. The point is not to dictate one policy or the other—to strap people to hospital beds or herd them into hospice—but instead for everyone to have choices and skin in the game.

By skin I mean money. If you choose hospice care and save your insurer or Medicare $100,000, why shouldn't some of those savings come back to you, or to your heirs?

A politician who suggested this would be tarred and feathered, and accused of paying people to die. Yet that type of thinking shows how thoroughly our dysfunctional system has played with our minds. It assumes that the most important decisions about our health are in the hands of politicians and regulators, and that the money belongs to the government. It also assumes that their values and judgments suit all of us, that our funds in this case should be spent on hospitalization and frightening, expensive (and often painful and futile) heroic measures. It is our right to have this treatment. And it is also our obligation, as a society, to pay for it.

Yet if we regard ourselves as shoppers, why shouldn't we be able to spend the money as we see fit? In this case, we don't have the money in hand. So how about this hypothetical option? If you agree at age sixty-five to spend your last months in hospice care instead of a hospital, an extra $200 per month for the length of your retirement will go into a fund for your heirs. For a person who dies in a hospice at age ninety, that fund would climb to $60,000—or $76,872 with compounded interest at 2 percent.

I mentioned this idea to my friend Charlie Baker, the former chief executive of Harvard Pilgrim Health Care. In his experience, many people who take a philosophical approach toward death, and reject heroic measures in principle, are likely to ask for all the help they can get once they see their own death approach. This is human nature.

And in the case of patients with reduced coverage, who would have the nerve to hold them back? Can you imagine the news coverage?

Perhaps in such a case, the patient could simply forfeit the accumulated fund, leave the hospice, and receive care at a hospital. But the decision would likely spur the family to press the hospital on what they'd be getting for that $76,000. It would involve weighing risk and demanding accountability—value for the money invested. This doesn't happen enough in health care today.

I'm not expecting bold policy shifts on death, at least not any time soon. But still, if you carry the same idea—the freedom to choose— into other areas of our health, we could do far more to tailor health care to our preferences and personal budgets.

One model for what's wrong is cable TV. Most households in America pay around $80 per month for a dizzying selection of programming. We all get hundreds of channels. We flip through them, seeing chefs flattening crepes, lions mauling wildebeests, politicians filibustering, Koreans, Chinese, and Mexicans all speaking their languages, on and on, until we find the football game or movie we were looking for. Most people, I'd bet, spend almost all of their viewing hours on five or six channels. Yet we all have to pay for hundreds. What gives?

It's an artificial economy in which we all pay to protect scores of channels that presumably would fail on their own. Needham & Company, an industry research firm, estimates that if we were free to pick our channels à la carte, only twenty would survive. And the cable industry would lose $70 billion in annual revenue. For some, that's a scary prognosis.

I say, let's give it a go. Let's trying focusing on what we really want, and not what we're forced to buy, and see what happens. Yes, maybe every household will lose access to Korean-language programming. Maybe we'll lose *Bonanza* reruns and ten or fifteen of the Saturday football games. But these predictions, which might sound dire to some, fail to take into account a very big and important unknown: How will the market respond? If there are a million households in the country that want Korean programming, don't you think that someone somewhere will figure out how to sell it to them? And once that programming company focuses on a real market, maybe it can figure out what those viewers truly want and what they'll pay for. Instead of buying a lot of canned content from Seoul and accepting the monthly handout from the cable giants, the programmer can focus on paying customers and innovate.

I'll bet you can guess where I'm going with this. Yes, health insurance is sold like a super-duper cable subscription, in which we all buy a deluxe package, with sports galore, HBO, Showtime, you name it. We all pay for all of it, even the parts we don't want or need. And why is this? Why should fitness nuts pay for gastric-band surgeries? Why should devout Roman Catholics pay for birth control pills? Because policy makers have decided that we all have a right to the full package. Equally important, if we don't all pitch in, the less popular offerings—the health industry's version of Cozi TV and Azteca America—won't be able to sustain themselves.

So we all stick together and pay for every kind of surgery. This way, we avoid having to make difficult choices. Naturally, insurance is ridiculously expensive. And why wouldn't it be? Not only are we buying from a wasteful and morally paralyzed industry, but we're buying virtually *everything* it has to sell, even if we don't want or need it. Is it any surprise that millions of Americans either cannot afford such a package or choose not to buy one?

This issue arises at athenahealth. We have about three thousand employees. The most expensive thing we pay for is for three people a year to have in vitro fertilization and premature babies, often in multiples. Those procedures result in expenses topping $1 million. That's about $1,000 per employee. In an à la carte system, a handful of employees would pay extra for the in vitro option. It would be like subscribing to HBO, while others would save money by sticking to a smaller basic package.

In this case, there are solid arguments for us to pay the money. These women might reasonably point out that they devoted their most fertile years to building athenahealth. Now that we're a big company with a market capitalization in the billions, we can spend some of that money helping them have babies. Point taken.

But imagine if each of us could choose only the health insurance we wanted, à la carte. In such a scenario, maybe only twenty women in our whole workforce would be interested in the expensive in vitro coverage. And a good number of them would no doubt be driven away by the cost, which would presumably skyrocket once the vast majority of customers dropped it. Would that be the end of the story? A service that costs $1 million shrivels and dies for lack of paying customers?

I don't think so. But it would create a crisis for the in vitro providers. To save their business, they would have to get creative, finding ways to bridge the gap between their million-dollar service and potential customers. First, they'd cut costs. This might sound obvious, but it requires a 180-degree shift from their current business model, which is based on *cost padding*. The possible savings are immense. They'd eliminate superfluous testing, and replace surgeons at many steps in the process with nurses or technicians. They'd use scheduling software, and would haggle with suppliers. In short, they'd operate like a serious business. I have no doubt that they could cut their costs in half by just attacking the easy stuff, the low-hanging fruit. And this would come *before* they start innovating.

Next, they could reach out to potential customers. Could there be a way to make the financing easier? Perhaps they could amortize the investment over twenty years or offer rebates in cases where the procedure fails. Or maybe they could broaden the base of interested customers be-yond the women who are trying to have the babies. They're not the only ones invested in the process. Could they offer a reduction in rates if the insured got friends or family members to sign up for other options? This would turn their potential customers into marketers for the service, a strategy that cell phone providers use. (I'll admit, it might be obnoxious, but nothing compared to a million-dollar invoice.)

If you see what's happening in this hypothetical process, the price of in vitro fertilization is plunging and the industry is focusing on the cus-tomer, all because of one tough decision: to stop including this treat-ment in everyone's health insurance. Meanwhile, millions of people who don't opt for in vitro coverage would be saving perhaps a couple hundred dollars a year. That leaves more money in their pockets, per-haps to shop for something they really want—and not what they're told they have to buy.

In my vision, all of the health care packages get unbundled. People sign up only for the services they want. Healthy twenty-eight-year-olds might sign up only for catastrophic coverage, and shop for everything else. If they get into a car crash or are diagnosed with Hodgkin's dis-ease, they're covered. If they get a strep throat, maybe they spend $129 at an urgent care center. They'd have health care, but only the parts that they, guided by their human values, chose to include.

A minimal plan would put money into people's pockets, and en-courage them to take on more responsibility. From another perspec-tive, it would give them more freedom. Not all of the results will satisfy the medical establishment. Some people might skip the $200 trip to the dentist and spend the money instead on Yankees tickets, or to buy gro-ceries. Is that OK? For lots of people, it isn't. These well-meaning souls have studies that establish what's good for us, and they staunchly believe those tests and procedures should be included in everyone's plan. Legions of lobbyists heartily support these decisions.

I was hoping against hope that Obamacare would provide cut-rate choices with high deductibles for people who want to shop. Maybe you'd pay half as much, be covered for the disasters, and foot the bill for everything else. This would create millions of new health care shoppers. To my disappointment, the new medical exchanges provide menus with choices in gold, silver, and bronze that are absurdly similar. None of them offers an option for the minimalist.

Offering a bare-bones plan, unfortunately, doesn't play politically. It sounds heartless. Here's Congress with its own deluxe all-you-can-eat health plan passing laws that seem to force the less fortunate to pay for their own pap smears and electrocardiograms. What cads! (And yes, I've got a similar problem, as a privileged CEO, calling for the same thing.) But driving more of health care into a competitive market is the only way to rescue and improve it for all of us.

The other argument against bare-bones plans is that we need those twenty-somethings to buy a full policy. Healthy young people, after all, must underwrite care for the rest of society, especially the sick and the elderly. But this funding hole exists only because "health care" has come to mean a full menu of exorbitant services delivered by an utterly uncompetitive industry. It doesn't have to be that way. To escape it, we have to think seriously about risk.

Picture a bus shelter on a city street. It starts to rain, and people gather underneath it. As the rain picks up, a growing crowd pushes and shoves to get under the tiny roof. It's uncomfortable. Someone has nasty BO. People can hardly breathe. What's more, the wind is whipping, and everyone is getting wet. But just imagine how much worse it would be to walk in the rain! More people jam in.

Then someone bolts. Look at him. He's standing out there in the rain, wet as can be, and he's smiling. He has made a choice, and it's not necessarily a bad one. What he has figured out is that the problem he was facing—call it "wetness," or perhaps "discomfort"—was not an either/or. The choice wasn't between comfort and safety under the crowded shelter, or disaster under the open sky. Comfort was on a continuum. Yes, he's getting soaked now. But he was getting pretty wet under the shelter, along with other unpleasantness there.

The key for us as a society, I believe, is to stop looking at health care, and the choices surrounding it, as binary choices: safety versus danger, coverage versus no coverage. Life doesn't exist in these extremes, but instead on a continuum. Risk is present in every scenario, and it's impossible to calculate for the individual. Let's say a person fortunate enough to have a platinum health plan goes to a hospital for an expensive test that someone with a stingier plan couldn't afford. Once he's in that hospital, he could be misdiagnosed and admitted, and he could wind up dead, either from a botched surgery or a hospital-borne infection. These things happen. A 2013 study published in the *Journal of Patient Safety* estimates that as many as 440,000 people die every year from preventable medical errors, mishaps like sponges left in wounds and babies getting grown-up doses of drugs. I don't say this to indict hospitals, but just to make the point that access to fully reimbursed hospitalization does not equal safety. It often represents a preferable option, and sometimes not. Like everything else, it entails a degree of risk. So does staying out of hospitals.

So how do we as individuals weigh those risks? How do the risks affect the choices we make? Well, if you look at the areas of our lives where we're free to make choices, we're all over the map. Millions choose to smoke cigarettes and eat bacon cheeseburgers. Others are vegans who drink bottled water and breathe filtered air. But some of them don't wear seat belts, or go bungee jumping in Borneo. I try to watch what I eat, but still don't hold a candle to my wife's self-control. I also ride my bike through the chaotic streets of Cambridge. Is that riskier than going ten years without an electrocardiogram or getting blood tests on a regular basis for signs of prostate cancer?

I don't know. There's risk in everything.

The danger is to clutch to the fiction that there exists in health care a single safe option, one that hews to one set of American Medical Association–endorsed procedures through which risk can be minimized. This type of thinking leads us to wrap health care in layers upon layers of protections. It's as if we all agreed to drive down a single "safe" road, and then brought in the Army Corps of Engineers and platoons of consultants, and spent astronomical quantities of time and money calibrating the banking on every curve and establishing peer-reviewed protocols for oil removal, traffic signaling, and drainage.

What's wrong with that? some might ask. It's the health of Americans we're talking about here. Shouldn't they get the best?

A couple of issues. First, not everyone will agree that the designated superhighway is the best. Maybe it's crowded. Maybe they don't want to pay for it, or they just don't like it. Maybe they prefer another road, or perhaps they're just feeling ornery. We're a wonderfully diverse nation and we'll naturally have an equally diverse range of opinions on what's "best." In any case, if one system is mandated, people lose the freedom to choose. The only options are more or less of the safe and approved system. That's not shopping.

Worse, the relentless focus on risk reduction in a single system stifles creativity. Consider NASA. The overriding goal in building the space shuttles was safety. The machine simply had to get astronauts up and back reliably. So engineers put together fabulously complex machines bristling with sensors and backup systems. They had no competition, so time to market wasn't an issue. Neither was the cost or, for that matter, innovation. The process for getting components and technologies approved was so exhaustive and expensive that plugging in a new component was usually out of the question. Too risky. The result? Our astronauts flew well into this century on 1970s technology. The total cost of the program was $209 billion, which comes to $1.55 billion for each of the fleet's 134 missions. Despite all the hard work and meticulous engineering, two of them ended in tragedy.

Compare that to consumer electronics. It's been a hotbed of innovation for decades, largely because companies are free to take risks and to fail. Prices have plummeted, and we all carry miracle machines in our pockets and purses.

Now it is true that the stakes in health care are higher. Apple's handheld fiasco of the 1990s, the Newton, wouldn't be so entertaining if people had died from it. But we also want to benefit from new ideas and breakthroughs, and not to have our health strapped into a risk-averse medical version of the space shuttle program. We cannot afford it and it can't evolve quickly and flexibly enough to serve our needs. In such scenarios, we are victims, not players in the game. We are neutered. Accepting risk, and making stark choices, is not only good for the economy. It's what human beings do.

CHAPTER TWELVE

■

Fast Data

Considering your own medical data, try answering a few questions:

1. What was your blood pressure this morning?
2. Which hospital in your area has (a) the lowest cost for emergency visits, (b) the best safety record, (c) the highest rating for customer service, (d) the most experience in cancer, heart disease, etc.?
3. Are you genetically at risk for breast or testicular cancer?
4. How many calories have you burned in the last week?

Within the next several years, answers to more of those types of questions will be easily available. New streams of information, from personal genomes to exercise gadgets, like the Fitbit, will be creating vast new pools of data, both for personal medical management and research. Eventually, tracking information on our own bodies and the health care choices we face will be as intuitive as clicking through the stocks in our 401(k).

But data in health care means a lot more than answers to simple questions. Data will change our understanding of health. Instead of a handful of test results and a smattering of annual measurements in a folder, health data will increasingly be something that we generate passively, day by day, almost the way we produce CO_2 or garbage. This data will flow, creating patterns and, if we choose, triggering alerts. The bigger change, however, is that much of the data will be generated, shared, and consumed outside of the medical establishment. It will be ours. We will use it to manage our own lives, and we will choose doctors and other professionals to guide us in this endeavor.

It's easy to get distracted by visions of data in health care and to ignore its first big job, which is to run a business efficiently. It involves scheduling customers, getting them the treatment they need, and getting reimbursed. This is fundamental. If an enterprise can quickly find the right information for each encounter, it can optimize resources, run more smoothly, and get paid. This much has been true since Babylonian accountants scratched out their records on clay tablets. What's different now is that once a business is up and running with modern digital data, those trickles of data become torrents. Then all kinds of exciting possibilities emerge along with, yes, serious questions about privacy.

The way I see it, we can expect three data revolutions in health care. The first wave helps medical practices and hospitals run their businesses efficiently. The data lets them see (often for the first time) what they're doing. It spotlights where they're wasting time, energy, and money. This process alone, while it sounds simple, promises to bring astounding efficiency gains to health care. The second stage, which we glimpsed at Hudson Headwaters, uses data to help with diagnoses and treatment, and to manage the health of a population. It backs up the doctor's informed gut intuition, which is still valuable, with science. This should result in immense qualitative gains.

In the third stage, we move from Big Dumb Medicine to Small Smart Medicine. For this, we look at all of society as a vast laboratory.

What are people doing? How are they eating and exercising? For the first time, we have the wherewithal to carry out research on how people live in the real world. How are the different medicines working? Maybe one medication works far better for certain age groups, or nonsmokers, or only for heavy drinkers. While historically we have approved only the medicines and therapies that are safe and work for all of us, we now have a chance to figure out the right medicines, diet, and therapy for each individual. The opportunities are near limitless.

The impact of these three revolutions on health care will be enormous, so big in fact that it's ridiculous for government officials and corporate accountants to be drawing up projections of health care spending in 2025 or 2030. These inevitably feature terrifying graphs showing the expanding health care industry consuming our entire economy. Such scary predictions are akin to using revenue numbers from the Yellow Pages in 1998 to predict the future of commercial search—this at a time when Google was already on the rise.

It is true that disaster awaits us if we resist all change and turn our backs on the three data revolutions. But we cannot afford to, and we won't. The only question in my mind is how many delays and how much pain we'll endure, and how many trillions of dollars we'll waste, before we let innovation flower in this field. Sooner or later, health care will be a changed industry with utterly different dynamics and pricing, and it will revolve around data.

That evolution from trickles to torrents of data has taken place at athenahealth. From our early days, in which data trickled in through a 9-kilobyte modem, we now receive clinical data on fifteen million people, and a hundred thousand doctor visits a day, along with the business data—invoices and payments—on three times that many. This is growing at a rate of 30 percent per year.

The key, though, is not the size of the data trove, but instead what can be done with it. (I should mention here that the handling of all of this data is rigorously managed, according to regulations governing the privacy of medical records. We're maniacal about this, and have to be. It's the heart of our business.) This data includes both the business and clinical sides. It gives us a look at every step of what is often a convoluted process, from the time a patient calls in with a problem, to the check-in, the assessment, the treatment and prescription, the invoice, and the result. It raises endless interesting questions. Does the patient call back a month later with the same issue, or a related one? Is there a geographic, gender, or socioeconomic bias to an ailment? If it's contagious, how fast is it spreading, and where?

This is an immense and growing laboratory. Consider the ongoing hubbub surrounding cholesterol-lowering drugs known as statins. Studies come out indicating that statins save lives. Others conclude that they are overprescribed. Guidelines are issued and, amid controversy, amended. As this debate rages, what are doctors and patients doing? We can look. We can find doctors who prescribe loads of statins, and others who don't. With time, we can compare the results—and share them, so that doctors and patients and researchers can all learn. Of course, we can break down these results by age, demographic group, geography, weight, and a host of risk factors. With this data in hand, doctors will eventually be able to provide each patient with a risk score for taking statins. (How that risk plays out, of course, will always be a mystery. Statistics can guide our decisions, but each individual is unique.)

What's especially important is that this data is fresh and continuously flowing. It's happening now. It doesn't have to be cleaned and curated and passed through various supervisory panels. I can call up Josh Gray, our chief data researcher, and he can tell me how the flu season is progressing day by day in New Jersey. (If the curve looks like the monster flu season we had last year, I should probably get a shot.)

We can also analyze how people take or ignore their prescription drugs. So-called prescription noncompliance is a major problem. Many people forget to take their medicine, or get their pills confused. This can be dangerous, or even fatal, for patients. And it also pummels the economy. About one of every five people admitted to a hospital is readmitted within thirty days, according to a study by the Department of Health and Human Services. Naturally, this drives up hospitalization expenditures, which already devour about as much of our gross national product as the Department of Defense. Many of the readmissions can be traced to people not taking the right medicine.

Our data might be able to help. We can see the medicines that were prescribed, when those prescriptions are refilled, and when the patients return to the doctor with the same symptoms. Those are important pieces of the puzzle. By adding demographic data and health status to the mix, we might be able to pinpoint the patients most likely to need help with the medications. And then we can begin working with our clients to deliver different types of alerts. Does an occasional phone call help? A home visit? A text message? With enough data, we can try different approaches simultaneously on different groups of people. Maybe some messages are stern while others cajole. Others might provide data. They compete against each other. The more effective ones prevail in this Darwinian system, and through continuous competition the winners are honed for specific regional and demographic niches.

In marketing, this method is known as A/B testing. Some call them horse races. Every time you empty the mailbox and throw out a handful of credit card offers, you're participating in one of these horse races. The banks or phone companies are trying one approach on you, and your nonanswer closes the feedback loop for them. Next time maybe they'll try a bigger envelope, or a brighter font. Search engines like Google use a similar approach at warp speed as they size us up for online ads. Now it's just a question of expanding similar testing in health care. No statistical approach can be right all the time. But if this use of A/B testing reduces the national rates of medical noncompliance, it saves heartbreak for thousands of families—and cuts billions from our national health care bill.

Another project that intrigues me concerns how much time people wait at the doctor's office. Waiting is one of the hidden costs of health care. It's not just a matter of killing time in uncomfortable chairs with soap operas blaring. People often have to take time off from work, or hire a babysitter. Some drive through heavy traffic, in both directions. Their time is money, and it represents an uncounted health care expense—on top of the trillions that we get billed for.

Our data scientists can capture the elapsed minutes between the moment a patient signs in and the consultation begins. That's the waiting time. Then, conceivably, we'll be able to look for correlations between waiting time and other behaviors. Do offices where patients wait for more than thirty minutes suffer from higher customer churn? Are patients more likely to postpone or cancel visits when the wait is too long? Which types of visit, on average, take more time? Which patients take longer than their allotted fifteen or twenty minutes? Once these numbers are known, perhaps medical practices could book certain visits for a few extra minutes, and reduce wait time.

Airlines have recently used this type of analysis to optimize booking and scheduling, which is why most of the flights you take nowadays are full. And you can bet that Starbucks knows exactly how much more time it takes a barista to whip up a double mocha skim latte than an ordinary cup of joe. That type of data drives staffing decisions, which are focused on customer satisfaction and financial return. Similar data, increasingly, will be informing medical practices. And they'll need it— the sooner, the better—to keep up with the newcomers storming into the industry, such as the FastMed and MedExpress urgent care centers. Those outfits have run on data from day one.

Doctors, in one way or another, have always been in the data business. They've long kept records on height and weight, illnesses and medicines prescribed. Further, a big part of a doctor's job is to pick up data the old-fashioned way—to see, touch, smell, hear, and listen—and then to incorporate these learnings with formal knowledge. Even today, when a family doctor sticks in a tongue depressor and gazes down a person's gullet, he or she is gathering visual data, and matching it to images of strep throat and tonsillitis archived in memory. In coming years, computers like IBM's *Jeopardy* program, Watson, might increasingly be on doctors' call, plowing through voluminous records and reports, issuing alerts about certain combinations of medications and coming up with possible diagnoses. However, when it comes to analyzing the diverse signals coming from a single patient, there is still no computer or data analysis that can match a human mind endowed with the knowledge and experience of a doctor.

Yet even the best doctors could use some help from data. Sometimes the data we're talking about can be surprisingly small. Let's say, for example, that we come up with simple questions for patients. One of them might be, "Is it pretty easy for you to walk a mile?" Another might concern bedtime or the usual breakfast menu. Good doctors have been using this approach for centuries. They ask questions and note changes. But each doctor might have a different method, and until now there has been no way to test the thousands of possible questions and find the most effective. Through the analysis of petabytes of data, we should be able to come up with simple questions that establish a telling baseline for different types of patients. And at the point that the patient reports changes, either in person or online, then it might be time for tests.

In this case, the one fact would signal bigger trouble. It reminds me of a story I heard about Eddie Van Halen, the 1980s rock guitar legend. When his band toured, they carried around huge truckloads of speakers, fog machines, and other paraphernalia, including 850 PAR lamps. Assembling this electric extravaganza was a huge challenge. It often took nine or ten hours. For safety alone, the setup had to be perfect. The contract, according to the lead singer, David Lee Roth, was "thick as a Chinese phone book" with technical specs. And it was Roth who placed one unusual demand in the middle of the contract. It stipulated that promoters had to supply bags of M&M candies backstage for the band, and that none of these bags could include brown M&Ms. If even one brown M&M was to be found, the promoter would forfeit his entire share for the concert.

This sounded like Cleopatra ordering a slave to peel her a grape. Diva behavior. But it had to do with quality control. If the promoter's team ignored the M&Ms, it was probably missing other more important details as well. There was a likely correlation. And since Van Halen's band didn't have the time or expertise to inspect each one of the electric circuits, they found one simple test to set off an alarm. The bags of M&Ms were canaries in a coal mine.

In a similar way, data might help doctors come up with simple and effective questions. The prime encounter can and should still feature the doctor meeting with the patient the old-fashioned way, using all of those human attributes that machines cannot match. But the doctor, at the same time, can benefit from the knowledge gathered by thousands of other doctors facing similar cases. That comes from digital data. And in the best of cases, that wealth of knowledge will be distilled into a few simple and incisive guideposts and questions.

Data can also provide focus and context to the annual checkup. Millions of Americans with reasonably good health and standard insurance typically go for checkups once a year. If you think about those twenty-minute or half-hour sessions, the doctor or nurse practitioner first goes through a checklist, from the scale to the blood pressure, then a look in the ears, down the throat, and so on. It might not be until the final minutes that the visit gets customized, that the doctor talks to the patient about specific issues that may have emerged in the last year.

As population health management, this isn't too far removed from how a veterinarian manages farm animals. We're rounded up once a year and run through the standard checklist. What's more, as if we were illiterate beasts, the data from these encounters is often hidden from us. This is Big Dumb Medicine.

One important shortcoming in this approach concerns time. The checkup takes a snapshot from a single day, and it relies on people's faulty memories to account for the other 364. Let's say for a few days in November you experienced an occasional heart flutter. Then it went away. Will you remember to tell the doctor about this during your thirty-minute checkup in April? Maybe that bit of data, which should trigger a battery of tests, doesn't get picked up.

With the growth of digital technology, the standard once-a-year checkup will soon be seen as laughably primitive. We'll be surrounded by data about today, and yesterday, and last week. You can get a glimpse of this in Portland, Oregon, where Intel, the giant chip maker, has been working on health surveillance with scores of willing elderly couples. The project involves wiring these people's homes with every conceivable kind of sensor. These record the daily pathways through the house, the strength of each voice, the sleeping patterns and bathroom patterns. Sensors under the kitchen floor even report on how each person distributes his or her weight while cooking or washing dishes. All of this data goes to Intel computers, which establishes a baseline pattern for each couple.

The idea is that the computer will send alerts when it notes changes in these patterns. In the early days, it simply sends the news to human health care providers. But in time, the system itself will suggest possible causes for the change. A voice that loses strength, for example, could be an early sign of Parkinson's. A shift in weight distribution on the kitchen floor might signal muscle atrophy in the legs, which could lead to a fall—a major risk as we grow older.

You might wonder why a company like Intel would be researching health care. Let me answer that with a question: Do you spend as much money as you used to on computers? Most of us don't. But we have more computerized tools and consumer electronics in our lives, from cell phones to our cars. The challenge for Intel and other computer companies is to find new areas of our lives ripe for computing—and to colonize new industries. Here health care represents a mouthwatering market opportunity. That's why Google, Microsoft, Facebook, and loads of smaller companies keep prowling in the vicinity, looking for their niche.

Two things happen when consumer electronics crash into an industry. First, it starts gushing loads of digital data. Second, as any musician or journalist will tell you, services that used to cost a lot get cheap in a hurry, or even free. This is just starting to happen to health care, which is one reason all these projections about skyrocketing spending levels a decade or two from now are worthless. Another phenomenon when affordable consumer electronics and services show up in markets is that people buy them.

As this happens, more of health care will lend itself to shopping. Instead of today's dreary standard—something you have to pay for—more of the focus will shift toward something you want to buy. Today, the acquisitive health care shoppers have limited choices. Sure, they can buy better eyes (through LASIK), different noses, fuller lips, and trimmer waistlines through cosmetic surgery. They can trade in old knees and hips for upgraded models. And they can download apps to watch their weight or chart their biking routes. But the overwhelming spend falls into that black hole of insurance premiums and co-pays, which feel less like shopping than taxes. As consumer electronics pushes into the market, that will change.

And we'll be under higher levels of surveillance. To be sure, not too many of us are likely to be digging up our kitchen floors to install sensors or importing electronic toilets from Asia. Much of the surveillance data will be little data, not big. In other words, while computers might eventually be sorting through petabytes of our sensor data to sniff out possible maladies, that's probably a decade off for the mainstream population. The market for health surveillance today is much simpler: Did Grandmother in Kansas get out of bed this morning? Supplying that one nugget of information is medically valuable and can create a market. People will pay for it.

One of the sensors in Intel's Portland project fits this mold. A simple scale in the bed sends the doctor the person's weight every night. It's small data, but vital. For someone with congestive heart troubles, a sudden gain in weight can signal the gathering of fluids in the lungs. Both the doctor and patient should know this promptly, and respond to it. Even simple data like this, though, can be misinterpreted. In one case, computers concluded that a woman had gained eight pounds, when in fact her dog had jumped up on the bed.

As this technology spreads, we'll increasingly find ourselves tracking and measuring our lives—and at the same time being tracked and measured by others. Surveillance is well under way as people seek to protect those they're responsible for: their young children and elderly parents. This generates health data. Smart baby monitors now track infants' movements, their sleeping and eating patterns, and alert parents to changes. At the same time, baby boomers are wiring their parents' homes with surveillance cameras and fall-detector technology.

This type of technology, it's worth noting, is valuable for our health as well as our economies. The graying populations in the industrialized world, including the United States, are living into their nineties and beyond. These economies cannot afford to house tens of millions in assisted living, and they will look to technology to help people stay for longer in their own houses and apartments. This is critical in aging populations such as Japan's and Italy's. But it will also be important in the relatively more youthful United States as tens of millions of baby boomers start cycling through geriatric wards. (You'll know this seismic shift is approaching when you start to hear Led Zeppelin rocking the nursing homes and rehab centers.)

As we adapt more of these tools and services, we'll be generating rivers of health-related data. They'll make the puny notes in the doctor's office today seem pathetic in comparison. The use of these surveillance tools raises no end of privacy questions. But people will share their personal data, just as we do in finance and education, when we're convinced that it is in secure hands and that we're getting something of value for it.

The growth of 24/7 data will transform heath care, and also insurance. Already, auto insurance companies, such as Progressive, are offering special deals to drivers who agree to put a black box in their cars. That way they can track driving patterns, jackrabbit accelerations, and speeding after midnight, and eventually charge drivers for their individual risk—and stop insuring people as herds.

With the expansion of health data, insurance carriers will increasingly be in a position to offer customized rates. Consider a person with diabetes who installs a glucose monitor. This involves implanting a tiny monitor under the skin, which measures glucose levels and interacts with the insulin pump. This data is transmitted, though radio signals, to a nearby monitor and, if necessary, through the Internet to a caregiver. It won't take too many years for insurance carriers to calculate the difference in claims between those who use this technology and those who don't. And once they know that number, won't they lower rates for people who share monitoring data? I imagine someone will.

And then what about the marathoners or swimmers who accumulate loads of biological data? Many start with a Fitbit or Jawbone wristband to track the miles run and calories burned. But then they see the possibility of measuring sleep, diet, anxiety—in short, participating in what's called the "Quantified Self" movement. These people are hard at work attempting to optimize their health. Aren't they likely to flock to doctors, and to insurance companies, that welcome this data and use it to give them better service and care?

At the same time, as I mentioned earlier, different blends of data, including patient behavior, genetics, location, and weather, should enable researchers to study the effects of certain drugs and regimes in the wild. This could lead to immense widening of care, opening all kinds of possibilities that are now feared, forbidden, or unknown and unimagined. Consider the constricted possibilities given to us by Big Dumb Medicine. A pharma giant must spend an average of $350 million to get a single drug through a regulatory process that drags on for twelve years. It involves a year of Phase 1 testing, usually with a group of sixty to one hundred patients, to see if the drug is safe and what the side effects are. Next, in Phase 2, they test to see if the drug works for the targeted disease. That phase can take up to two years. It is followed by Phase 3, in which they test a larger group of people for longer, up to three years. Then they carry out more tests to figure out dosages and messaging, and how to market the medicine.

This is government looking out for people—and squashing innovation. I can see where the safety testing is valuable. But once certain drugs are deemed safe, how about letting the patients experiment with a few of them? We already do something very much like this, on a massive scale. Every day millions of people reach into the cabinet and take a drug against doctor's orders. In a 2013 Reuters survey, one in ten Americans admitted to taking medicine prescribed for others, usually to deal with pain, nausea, or insomnia, or in about one third of the cases, to get high.

Now, how about if we turn people loose to take a few of the medicines they choose and encourage them to report results? For many, the first response to this idea will be laughter or outrage. And experts no doubt will be able to cite examples where such an initiative would be downright dangerous. But instead of focusing on cases where it won't (and shouldn't) work, how about thinking of others where it might? If we allow for some experimentation, we will likely find that certain medications work against diseases and conditions they weren't designed for. Yes, it might only be for a minority. But the point isn't to find drugs that work for everybody. That's the claustrophobic world of Big Dumb Medicine. If a drug works for certain people, or under certain conditions, researchers combing through the data should be able to identify niche markets for it. Think of the possibilities. For every medicine that makes it from the laboratory to the pharmacy shelf, 999 fail, some of them in the second, third, or fourth stage of testing—in other words, after being deemed safe. Some of those drugs too could be placed on the market, where consumers participate in a kind of informal laboratory. This could be one of the pathways leading toward personalized medicine.

A lot of those researchers will be amateurs, compiling data on wikis, writing their conclusions on blogs, or debating them on social networks. In this way, they will not only carry out the experiments but also handle lots of the research and analysis. (They won't replace all of the professionals, but will force them to adapt to a widening market.)

Engaged health care citizens will also be researching hospitals and urgent care centers. Like blogging, this process will produce mistakes, exaggerations, and lies, but also valuable insights. The result will be that millions of us will participate in figuring out our health, taking control of it and responsibility for it. Our experience of health care will be widened and transformed. The industry will feel like it's ours, because it will be.

CONCLUSION

Where Do We Go from Here?

For too long, we've regarded health care in America as a problem or, worse, a crisis. Yes, the industry is awash with serious issues. It would be foolish to argue otherwise. But each one of those problems represents an opportunity. If there is one central message to this book, it is this: We are standing on the edge of a great opportunity. This is true not just for entrepreneurs, but for all of us, for patients and doctors and folks who work in government. All of us have the chance to participate in a renaissance of health care in America. Not all of the answers will be easy. Not all will be popular. As in any competitive industry, many companies and venerable institutions, big and small, will go belly-up. But this is a good thing, because failure represents risks taken, and new opportunities opening up for others.

The time has come for literally millions of people to reinvent health care. We can transform it from an increasingly monolithic and inhuman bureaucracy into a flourishing marketplace, one in which we're free to make our most important decisions. It is in deciding how to manage our health—the most serious decision we engage in—that we can truly express our humanity. At the same time, this market will allow a broad range of people, from doctors and nurses to entrepreneurs, not only to do good, but also to do well.

In concluding this book, I'll lay out some advice for different groups, many of them overlapping (since everyone is a patient at some point).

What Should Government Do?

It would be easy to say simply, "Get out of the way." Many people would leave it at that. But since the government runs about half of the health care economy and regulates the other half, getting completely out of the way is not a viable option—nor one I consider safe. The more important question is what governments can do to encourage competition and innovation in health care. In some cases, this does involve getting out of the way. The issue is where and how. In other areas, you might be surprised to hear me say, government could actually do *more*.

Let's start, though, with areas in which less is the goal.

1. Make room for the crazy ones

Government officials often say, "We want to work with business." They mean it. Baked into that statement, however, is a dangerous and naive assumption: that the government knows how to negotiate with all of the players in the industry.

That's impossible. How about the entrepreneurs who are just putting together their disruptive business plans? They aren't represented. In fact, the only people at the table, invariably, are those with enough scale to be seen, which also means that they already have a large business making money from the status quo. Their natural inclination is to steer clear of the disruption the whole system desperately needs. They want nothing to do with the kooks.

To be fair, I should add that I've spoken in Washington at a government-sponsored gathering called Datapalooza. It's teeming with start-ups. But it felt like walking onto the set of a Sacha Baron Cohen movie. A huge number of the "entrepreneurs" were Beltway Bandits eager to learn the Maximum Leader's latest dance move. ("Haven't you heard?" you could almost hear them saying. "We are all supposed to be entrepreneurs now.") True, there were also plenty of real start-ups in that assembly hall. But even if the government opens its doors to entrepreneurs, there's no way to give them all a seat at the table, or to hear their voices.

So how can the government listen to and support them? My advice is to create conditions for start-ups to take root and prosper. As they grow and disrupt, they'll make their voices heard in the marketplace. That's where the drama should be taking place, not in Washington and state capitals.

2. Trim the antikickback laws

Let's consider a truly nasty kickback. A contractor who wants to build a $100 million bridge pays $1 million to a few officials on the highway commission. This way, he manages to bypass the bidding process and win the contract. The harm to the public is clear. Competing contractors, who might have built a better bridge for less money, are denied the chance to bid.

We certainly don't want deals in health care where two interested parties are quietly negotiating mutual benefits at the expense of the patient. The antikickback laws attempt to address this issue. They prohibit payments, direct or indirect, that would induce patients to buy any products or services payable by a federal health care program, such as Medicaid and Medicare. This includes doctor referrals. Like most laws, it seems to make sense. Imagine an unscrupulous doctor giving patients twenty-dollar coupons for unnecessary and overpriced CT scans at his brother-in-law's imaging shop. We don't want Medicare paying for that.

But how about this scenario: An ophthalmologist needs medical records for a diabetic patient she's about to operate on. She can ask the patient's doctor for them, but according to the law, he must provide them for free. She cannot reimburse him, say, $5 for the trouble. That would constitute a financial relationship between the two parties, which could run afoul of the antikickback laws. The result is that doctors have no financial incentive to build up their information operations. (Instead of providing free referrals, it's worth noting, many are now accepting employment at hospitals in exchange for access to their customers. This, it could be argued, is a form of kickback.)

The government has done good work in protecting people's rights to data and defending privacy. But it has inadvertently gotten in the way of a functioning market for data. In such a market, parties are free to reimburse each other for information. That creates incentives for caregivers at every level to invest in their data and to provide prompt service. Data becomes an integral part of the business, a potential source of revenue. Think of landing in Paris, or Singapore, and being able to access an American bank account through an ATM. Banks pay each other to provide this service, and even hit up customers for a few bucks. We may grumble, but it's a functioning data business.

We deserve nothing less for health information. After all, it's in our best interest for the doctors treating us to have the most relevant and up-to-date information. Many of us will want access to it ourselves, and even be ready to pay for it.

Would you be willing to pay, say, $9.99 for a health app that keeps and updates all of your medical records, and permits you to search medications or maladies either chronologically or by keyword? I'm betting a lot of people would.

In a vibrant health data market, serving up such apps could be a big business. Will there be abuses? No doubt. As in every data market, mismanagement in some quarters is inevitable. So are invasions of privacy and other headaches. But we already have strong legislation on the books, including the 1996 Health Insurance Portability and Accountability Act (HIPAA). The best policy is to adjust regulations after new problems emerge, not by disabling the market from the get-go.

3. Right to work, right to shop

In a number of municipalities, including New York City, taxi drivers need a license issued by the city—a medallion—to do their job. This presumably protects passengers, limiting cabs to licensed and identifiable cars. But the number of these medallions is limited. The result is an artificial market of haves and have-nots. In an auction in late 2013, medallions for the first time sold for more than $1 million.

What would these medallions be worth if anyone with a driver's license and a car could operate as a taxi? This is starting to happen as citizen-cab services like Uber enter the market. But the standard cabs have paid a lot of money to have the market to themselves. So it was little surprise in 2013 that a new ride-sharing service, Sidecar, got a rough reception in New York. Two of the drivers were detained, and one had her car impounded. The cabdrivers, in a sense, are a protected guild, free of the competition that might benefit the public.

Health care is chockablock with artificial barriers like this to protect incumbents from competitors. Endless credentials and licensing requirements ensure steady work for one guild or another, often when a lowlier order could do the job just as well, or even better, at a lower price. All of these groups have their lobbyists working to keep the regulations in place, and to preserve their market. The medical schools participate as well by limiting the supply of each specialty.

The insiders invoke safety and quality of service to defend these rules. But when we were running our birthing business, I saw firsthand how such rules were used to keep highly qualified midwives at bay. They threatened the guild.

Certain licensing requirements still make sense. Anesthesiologists come to mind. But many of the licensing regulations just get in the way. Medical professionals should be able to establish their value and authority by the work they do, not the regulations protecting them. A freer marketplace would provide more competition, more choice, and higher-quality service—and at lower prices.

State governments could also offer their citizens a big favor by letting them shop for insurance across state lines. Why not? Information travels across states lines. So do dollars. Are these laws protecting their citizens or a handful of companies with strong lobbying operations?

In the same vein, some state governments often prohibit new businesses, like medical imaging start-ups, from setting up. The reason: They don't want "oversupply." Such regulations, much like New York's taxi medallions, protect incumbents and punish consumers. This is an easy one. Open the industry to newcomers and let the market choose the winners.

4. Expand Medicare Advantage

The goal should be to put business, wherever possible, between the government and the patient. Medicare Advantage is a prime example. In this program, a private insurer receives a set amount of dollars for each customer, and then figures out how best to deliver the necessary care. This is known as a capitated plan. When it works well, the insurer shops. The program currently staggers under way too much red tape, and in many states it sinks back into the standard fee-for-service model. But if the government could push Medicare Advantage as a true capitated plan, it would represent a meaningful step toward a market economy. The next step, of course, would be to share savings with the customers, and to give them more freedom to pick the levels of insurance they want. But for now, I'll stick with a simpler plea: Fix Medicare Advantage, and expand it.

5. A Fannie Mae for new health insurance start-ups

One big problem is that there are only a handful of mega-insurance carriers, and all of them basically offer the same package. There's very little experimentation. What we need are lots of insurance start-ups that can try different schemes. The trouble is that an insurance start-up would need to launch with about a million customers to have the necessary scale to cover risk. Think about it. If you have an insurance company that covers only ten thousand people, a disproportionate run of multimillion-dollar payouts sinks the business. Once it gets closer to a million customers, the risk statistics even out.

This is one area where the government could help, perhaps the way it does with Fannie Mae and Freddie Mac in real estate. This entity would offer financing or guarantees for insurance start-ups and then pull it back as they get closer to a viable scale.

6. Don't dwell too much on tort reform

For more than a generation, doctors and politicians have called for limits on malpractice lawsuits. And there certainly have been abuses in the area. The risk of malpractice suits drove up insurance premiums for many doctors. I certainly witnessed it in the birthing business. But malpractice suits have been declining for the last decade, and premiums are inching downward.

What's more, as digital medical records become the norm, doctors will have clear records of what they have done. As more of the basic information of care is reliably captured electronically, clinical decision support can be more easily deployed in the large portion of health care where there are definitive right answers. (Those who don't bring care under control should pay more to stay in business.) Workflow documentation will eliminate much of the doubt around treatment, which is precisely what fuels legal action.

What Should Doctors Do?

Doctors are very special and they should focus on doing work that no one else can do. The goal for the doctor is to spend as much time as possible focusing his or her attention, knowledge, and intelligence on diagnosing and treating patients. For this to happen, doctors have to manage their affairs intelligently. This involves delegating as much of the work as possible to collaborators, including nurses and medics, and using technology to gather resources and handle the busywork. For their happiness, prosperity, and the good of society, doctors must learn to manage their resources for the twenty-first century. They have to think like entrepreneurs.

1. Take risks

Increasingly, the new focused factories in medicine are going to address specific ailments and conditions, like replacing knees or clipping out colon polyps. Those easily repeated interventions will increasingly become commodity treatments, and the businesses will grow around efficiency and customer service. Trained aides and nurses will shoulder more and more of the work in such shops. Machines will handle more of the precision work and administrative chores. A few doctors will sit atop these systems, overseeing operations and intervening in the more complicated cases. But the greater opportunities will come from the bigger picture. More than a technician or a scientist, the successful doctor in coming years will be a provider. This means taking responsibility not just for one episode of care, but for the entire continuum.

An orthopedic surgeon, for example, might move beyond hip replacement and instead sell an entire mobility service. This would cover everything from the first consultation with a bedridden patient through an operation and rehab—and perhaps even having an associate trading tips and updates with her as she trains for the Boston Marathon. Instead of replacing a broken component, the doctor is selling a service involving product management.

This changes the economics. Increasingly, doctors who package integrated services will be able to sell them for a fixed price, buying risk.

Once they do this, they become medical providers. This might include a concierge service that gives patients answers and advice, and guides them through their surgery and recovery. A crucial component is shopping, because to make money the doctor will scout out the best and most cost-effective focused factories, imaging centers, physical therapists—whatever it takes. In this way, doctors will become the first wave of shoppers in the new health care industry. And with risk contracts, good shopping will help them make money.

Smart doctors, of course, won't be shopping alone. They'll be in touch, helping each other find the best deals, and also negotiating as groups.

2. Organize instead of selling out to hospitals

The health care industry is in transition, and it can look frightening. When a hospital official knocks on the door with a big check in hand, it must be tempting. It's no surprise that tens of thousands of doctors have exited private practices to become hospital employees in the last decade.

But doctors have to realize that they hold the cards, and that hospitals are anything but safe havens. Many of the hospitals eager to hire them are in rough shape. They run inefficient businesses in an industry with too much capacity. Empty beds spell ruin. To stay alive, they need to sell overpriced services and procedures to a steady stream of patients, and for access to these patients they need the doctors.

Not to put too fine a point on it, but doctors can either take refuge in these struggling businesses that resist consolidation by jilting their patients—not the best long-term strategy, I'd say—or they can join together with each other and provide excellent service to patients, and create thriving businesses from it. This way they profit from forcing the consolidation of hospitals, a strategy aligned with society's interests.

3. Get connected

Doctors should use the Internet, and insist that everyone they work with does, too. It's insane that I am writing this in the second decade of this century, but for some, the message has still not gotten through.

Increasingly, doctors are going to be operating in an ecosystem teeming with information about patients, populations and health issues. It will be crucial to gain access to every stream of information, especially as they take on risk contracts. Just like other entrepreneurs, doctors will need the data to tell them how their product is performing. This means establishing feedback loops, comparing results, and using them to optimize operations. In this sense, successful doctors will be running data laboratories that follow patients everywhere they go, even to competing institutions. The best ones already do.

What Should Entrepreneurs Do?

First, entrepreneurs have to confront an unwelcome reality: Facebook exists and has gone to market. Same goes for Twitter, Google, and LinkedIn, not to mention outfits like Microsoft and Apple. What does this mean? In the world of big consumer applications for technology, the low-hanging fruit has been plucked. Sure, other breakthroughs are inevitable. But the competition is sure to be tough, coming from start-ups and titans alike.

The health care economy, by contrast, is a jungle dripping with low-hanging fruit. The opportunities are limitless, and the market is immense. For digital entrepreneurs, it's almost like getting a chance to return to 1998. So the first thing they should do, after the requisite due diligence, is to jump in.

One great advantage of plunging into health care is that the competition, in many cases, is *nonexistent.* In other words, customers, whether patients or caregivers, are getting by without the best service or software. They may be suffering long waits or communications snafus. But that suffering is the status quo. They're used to it. Let's say you come along with a solution and they don't like it. At that point in a normal market, you're dead. But in health care, there's often no competitor to sweep in. You can refine your product, come back again, and still find the potential customers suffering with the status quo, ready to be convinced. For those arriving from more competitive industries, the emptiness of the health care market can lead to slack-jawed disbelief. It's too good to be true.

There are reasons for this, of course. It's a convoluted industry full of roadblocks and regulations. Many of the customers are nonprofits, which are less than eager to buy disruptive technologies. And yes, the industry grapples with certain issues, like death, that require more serious reflection than, say, mobile video games. But at the same time, getting into health care provides entrepreneurs with a chance not just to build a thriving business, but to serve humanity. Here are a few examples:

1. Recurring revenue

Build technology-enabled services, not technology. This means selling the outcomes, and keeping the how-to mostly to yourself. Also, the cost of sale is so prohibitively high in health care that you need to keep getting revenue without going back for sales calls. This favors subscription models.

2. Connective tissue

Think of the various elements of the health care economy as islands. There's the doctor's office, ambulance service, hospital emergency department, imaging facility, rehab center, nursing home. I could go on and on. Each one is an island. Patients bounce back and forth between them, but their information, more often than not, stays behind. Ask anyone who has tried to manage communications among these islands. It's often rudimentary, fragmented, distorted, or misplaced, and sometimes nonexistent. And just imagine what it's like for a senior, who has serious health issues and may be growing forgetful.

Building links to connect and communicate with these islands is a massive opportunity for tech companies. An entrepreneur named Russ Grancy, for example, saw these needs when his uncle was getting discharged from acute care at a hospital. He had Alzheimer's and needed help. But it took seventeen phone calls, five faxes, and three extra days in the hospital to line it up. This led Graney to found Aidin. Think of it as Match.com for discharge planning professionals. Aidin is only one niche of hundreds.

This connective tissue is also an opportunity for providing the human touch. Take the example of Senior Bridge. Founded in 2000, the company trained and dispatched caregivers to the homes of seniors who needed help—help with managing their meds, setting up appointments, preparing food, rehabbing a broken hip, even writing e-mails to grandchildren. The market for this type of service, they quickly saw, was vast. The company grew to more than fifteen hundred care managers and $72 million in revenue by 2012, when Humana Inc. snapped it up for undisclosed millions.

Further opportunities for this type of business are limitless. Just think about how many people need help, and how many folks with good people skills would be ready to help them for $40,000 or $50,000 a year. This is the workforce that Rushika Fernandopulle draws from for his coaches at Iora. And these people can be trained, not to replace doctors, but to provide help for every disease and every condition. Think of people who cannot see a specialist, but are carrying around a crippling anxiety. Is a one-on-one $200 session the only way to get support? I bet that with the right training, someone with the friendliness and people skills of a Starbucks barista could provide a valuable service.

3. Think primitive

The key for technology entrepreneurs is to produce a product or service whose value can be communicated in a five-minute meeting. It doesn't have to be sophisticated. Primitive is better. It's cheaper and probably easier to learn. It gets in the door quicker, and it can develop inside the industry, adapting to real needs (and not what software designers imagine the real needs might be before they make their first sale). Once a primitive technology is hitched up to a subscription, the client base will pull the technology into higher levels of sophistication.

4. Team up

Entrepreneurs need to team up to make themselves heard in Washington and the state capitals and among prospective clients. The big players all have sophisticated lobbyists working on their behalf. They also have large sales staffs, with golf outings and jets on call to carry prospective clients to site visits. Entrepreneurs need a voice to advocate for disruptions that the economy and the health industry urgently need— the sooner, the better.

What Should Patients Do?

There's a certain freedom that children feel when grown-ups are talking. They don't have to tune in to the discussion, whether it's about work or politics or the problems with the car. They're not supposed to understand it, and they have no responsibility for it. They're being taken care of. Sometimes, though, those plans the grown-ups were hatching don't turn out so great. So eventually children start paying attention to grown-up talk, and participating. It's part of growing up.

There's a parallel to health care. The system is for the most part inscrutable, understandable only to insiders. If patients don't make a concerted effort, they can go through decades without deciphering the numbers and acronyms on lab results and invoices. (Why did that colonoscopy with polyp removal cost $19,438? You don't want to know.) And while much about health care often doesn't seem to make sense, and is often unpleasant, at least we're being taken care of. For those of us with decent health and insurance, things could be worse.

But this is the time, I'm hoping, that many of us look around, add up the numbers and the facts, and stop accepting this status quo. In short, it's time that as a society, and as individuals, we assert ourselves and push for what we want. This revolution I've been calling for in health care cannot be handed down to us by the government or doctors. They can attempt to read our minds and offer us a menu of ten options, or perhaps a hundred. But in the revolution I'm calling for, 330 million people will push for what they want, in every conceivable blend of price, convenience, security, and risk, and a market will grow to serve them. Change will come from each individual, each patient.

And what should we patients do? In a word, take control of our lives and our health. For this, we require knowledge. This means clear language from caregivers, and access to our data, as well as a plethora of data and measurements that we gather ourselves. With that knowledge, we must demand choices. Finally, taking control of our bodies and our lives involves accepting responsibility for the choices we make.

1. Learn

There used to be a time when someone with cancer felt very alone. Until a few decades ago, you weren't even supposed to talk about it. It was secret. So if someone was diagnosed with cancer or, for that matter, any other dreaded disease, there was little way to find others who were battling it and what they were learning. It was even hard to gauge which doctors within a day's drive had experience with it. Patients lived in an information vacuum.

That's no longer the case. Consider Ben and Jamie Heyward. A decade ago, when they found out that their brother Stephen was suffering from ALS, they launched a Web site called PatientsLikeMe. It's an online community in which patients can share tips, data, and experiences with others afflicted with the same disease. It provides patients day-to-day support and information. And data from the site may also prove valuable for researchers.

Sites like PatientsLikeMe represent a sea change from the days when people kept their illnesses secret. They also turn power upside down. Patients create their own information and share it with others—and it all happens outside the medical establishment.

And just imagine how networks like this can fuel the shopping revolution I've been calling for. Once patients are in communication, they can point each other to the doctors with the most experience in the field, to the best deals for prescription drugs. They can warn them about imaging centers with long waits, rude service, or inflated bills. Information creates a market, and patients can generate much of the information themselves.

2. Know your body

When I was growing up, mature adults went to the doctor for a checkup every year. That was being responsible. But a more responsible approach is to learn about your own body, to give yourself checkups.

Think about the various measurements the doctor takes. Much of modern medicine involves establishing a baseline with those numbers and then seeing, year to year, if there are changes. We can all do that ourselves. We should know our bodies, and if there's some change in the terrain, we shouldn't wait for the doctor to find it. Has your pulse changed in the last month?

3. Demand your data

It's yours, or should be. Any medical practice that keeps your data from you, whether on a computer hard drive or a paper binder, doesn't deserve your business. Some of this is simple logistics. If you were to have a medical problem on a snorkeling vacation, or in Vienna, how would that data get to the doctors who need it? For that matter, if you wanted to switch to a medical practice across town, would they get the data?

Beyond logistics is the simple issue of ownership. Everyone should own his or her health care data. After all, we've certainly paid for it. Owning it, maintaining it, deciding when to share it and with whom is both our right and responsibility.

A lot of what I've been writing about points toward the future. And the focus on digital data can make it sound like we're entering an entirely new world of health care. But I'm also interested in recovering an old part of health care that is in short supply: the intense one-on-one relationship between the doctor and the patient. As I mentioned in the introduction, this is the time when the doctor is focused entirely on the patient that the practice of medicine ceases to be a job, much less an industry. It is one human being serving another.

I'm often inspired by a painting called *The Doctor*, a favorite of the author Abraham Verghese. Painted in 1891 by Luke Fildes, it shows a doctor in a humble household focusing on a sick child. The doctor is leaning forward, his chin in his hand, concentrating on his patient. This is not a doctor who is numbly cranking through patient visits. The girl's father stands in the background. He entrusts the girl's life to this man, and the doctor is trying as hard as he can. He is 100 percent focused, emotionally and intellectually. As I see it, he has tried the medicines. (The empty jar on the table might represent big pharma.) They haven't worked. Now it's entirely up to him. He's not distracted by paperwork or Medicare codes or the risk of a malpractice suit. He is performing his most important job. If he were an athlete, you might say that he's in the "zone." He is present in heart and soul.

The challenge for us as a society is to free up doctors for more of these special moments. Move the scene in the painting into the twenty-first

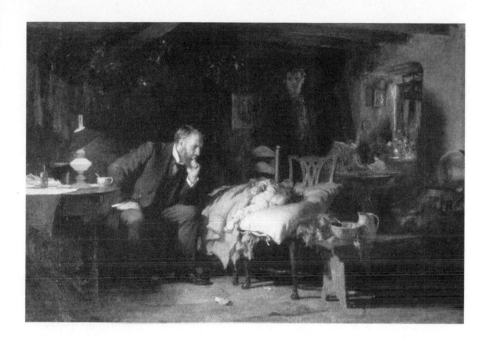

century and examine what is happening in the background. First of all, that doctor works in a medical practice that covers hundreds of patients, a good number of them with chronic diseases. Some of them are exchanging data with the office, while others are being cared for by medics or nurses, who make a lot less money than this doctor and have more time for noncritical cases. Meanwhile, a back-office provider is handling the administrative chores for this doctor. It's doing the work he hates— and freeing him up for the job he loves. In fact, every second he is distracted from this work, everyone loses: the doctor, the patient, and society.

Things have changed for the patient's family as well. They have studied their daughter's condition and are in touch with others who have the same disease, perhaps through new Web sites or social media. They exchange data with them, perhaps anonymously, if that's what their daughter prefers. They know this doctor has plenty of experience with the disease. They know how much he charges. They know a lot because they and the entire health care industry are now operating in the knowledge economy.

In short, they are participating in the health care revolution. It's actually pretty simple. They shop, they make choices, and they get the medical care they want and deserve. If we push for it, that's the way health care should be, and will be, for all of us.

ACKNOWLEDGMENTS

A book! This is a surprising project to emerge from the ADD likes of me, and yet here it is! The book's development has been one of the high points of my career thus far and it would never have happened without Steve Baker and my fellow *athenistas*. I walk around the earth with a fever . . . ideas and frustration burning all the time . . . and finally that heat has been channeled to real use, thanks to their combination of elegance, brilliance, and discipline. Let's be clear: Steve wrote this. I talked, ranted, interviewed, outlined, and edited, but Steve, with his master storytelling abilities, was able to turn my noise into music. Amazing, really.

Pierre Valette was the inspiration. He declared it worth doing and so we all started to find the time and thoughts and resources. John Fox was the general. An accomplished author in his own right, he found Jim Levine, our fantastic literary agent, who in turn led us to Steve Baker and to our dedicated publisher and editor at Penguin/Portfolio, Adrian Zackheim and Emily Angell. From there, John marched us through over a year's worth of writing sessions, pulling in the right people along the way to flesh out the story and to review the final product. Folks like Josh Gray, athenahealth's brilliant head of athenaResearch; Dan Haley and Dan Orenstein, our fearless government affairs leaders, who helped get the facts straight on policy and regulations; board members and true mentors Brandon Hull, Amy Abernethy, and Charlie Baker, who read drafts; Bob Kocher, who provided a thoughtful counterpoint to my nursed-at-the-right-breast views on government; and countless other colleagues are all due my thanks.

Our athenahealth clients fittingly became essential contributors and central characters in these pages. Athenahealth has over fifty thousand of them now and most all are inspiring. Ralph de la Torre, John Rugge, Ken Konsker, and John Briggs all give purpose and focus to my fevers by using the nascent health information backbone we are building to deliver better, more affordable care to their patients. John Randazzo and Rushika Fernandopulle (who are not clients, but should be!) continue to provoke and challenge us all to think differently about health care.

Atul Gawande, Clay Christensen, and Abraham Verghese are each, in my view, the deans of health care storytelling. I have learned and continue to learn so much in the presence of their ideas.

Finally, my original debt of gratitude, at the top of the debt food chain, goes to the original athenistas. Mitch Besser and the partners of Athena Women's Health and the Birthplace took an absurd risk entrusting their medical group to some kooky kids sharing laptops. I trust they are glad of the experiment. Ed Park, Leslie Brunner, Amy Pooser, Bob and Annie Gatewood, Andrea Nilsen, Jeremy Trelstad, Justin Lin, and Carl Byers, like Ernest Shackleton's crew heading to Antarctica, signed up for a "hazardous journey, small wages . . . constant danger, safe return doubtful, honor and recognition in case of success." The same goes for my original board members Larry Sosnow and Nancy Koehn (who educated me on Shackleton, among many other things). I'm sure I would never have survived the loneliest parts of this journey without such stalwart mates.

And of course, Todd. Todd Park is the greatest combination of heart and soul with brains and brawn I have ever known. He is an inspiration. Without Todd, there would be *nada*.

INDEX